Tol   **hy in**

Bu

citiz   **ar olds**

                                                           in the

P·C·P
Paul Chapman
Publishing

D1354523

Paul Chapman Publishing
A SAGE Publications Company
1 Oliver's Yard
55 City Road
London EC1Y 1SP

SAGE Publications Inc.
2455 Teller Road
Thousand Oaks, California 91320

SAGE Publications India Pvt Ltd.
B-42, Panchsheel Enclave
Post Box 4109
New Delhi 110 017

Commissioning Editor: George Robinson

Editorial Team: Mel Maines, Sarah Lynch, Wendy Ogden, Mike Gibbs

Designer: Jess Wright

A catalogue record for this book is available from the British Library
Library of Congress Control Number 2005932393

ISBN 1-4129-1307-1

Printed on paper from sustainable resources.
Printed in Great Britain by The Cromwell Press Ltd, Trowbridge, Wiltshire.

Contents

Preface

This is an activity-based teacher's guide to fostering positive group interaction through imagined experience and discussion at Key Stages 2 and 3. In a series of interactive workshops, each one providing a context, a scenario and a list of characters; pupils are invited to engage in discussion, debate and negotiation to solve problems and meet challenges. The primary focus at all times is the promotion of tolerance, empathy and cooperation, as prescribed in the programme of study and non-statutory guidelines for PSHE and Citizenship. Key transferable skills in oracy, enquiry and problem-solving are introduced and practised through each role-play, with specific links to the National Curriculum attainment targets for Speaking and Listening, and suggestions for extensive cross-curricular work.

How to Use the CD-ROM

The CD-ROM contains PDF files, labelled 'Worksheets.pdf' which consists of worksheets for each lesson in this resource. You will need Acrobat Reader version 3 or higher to view and print these resources.

The documents are set up to print to A4 but you can enlarge them to A3 by increasing the output percentage at the point of printing using the page set-up settings for your printer.

To photocopy the worksheets directly from this book, align the edge of the page to be copied against the leading edge of the copier glass (usually indicated by an arrow).

Introduction

Every class, regardless of size, can soon become entrenched in the dynamics of who is in charge, who is vulnerable, who steals the limelight and who shuns it. Qualities such as tolerance and empathy can be forgotten as stereotypes emerge and roles are forged in the melting pot of prejudices and preconceptions that accompany the introductions on day one. As Dornyei & Murphey (2003) suggest, in the early stages of a group's inception pupils observe each other suspiciously, sizing up one another and trying to find a place in an unestablished and unstable hierarchy. They are on their guard, carefully monitoring their behaviour to avoid any embarrassing lapses of social poise.

Once the die is cast, the resulting verbal and non-verbal interaction between group members may ensure that the hierarchy is maintained. For some this may mean a full script of opinionated speeches, emotive soliloquies and impassioned sermons at every available juncture; for others, the role of mute supporter may offer a smoother ride. Some will have earned (or been daubed with) the role of class jester, always ready with a quip and a palatable sound bite, but rarely taken seriously. Others may scoop the title of class spokesperson, or perhaps teacher's 'pet'. Whichever way the script is written, the characters cast and the blueprint for a child's language learning and personal and social development is drawn. Then, once this body of disparate roles has found a way of functioning together and an enforced cohesion has emerged, we, as teachers, set about promoting the importance of tolerance and empathy. We begin teaching Citizenship.

Our favoured tool for delivering a Citizenship curriculum is discourse; we strive to maintain clear lines of communication between ourselves and our pupils, and between the children themselves. We believe we are acting as facilitators for free thought and expression. We like meritocracies; we favour no-one. The vision we hold for an equitable and harmonious society is modelled in the microcosm that is our classroom. Tolerance and empathy, core skills in the citizenship curriculum, are 'taught' through controlled group discussion and teacher led debates. If a child is quiet in the discussion we invite him to speak. If a child is too loud, we seek to restrain her. We pacify and we accommodate; our goal is an equable discourse, but a quiet room will do.

Yet beneath the communication systems of a teacher-led citizenship lesson, there lies a different discourse – a language of social trends, fashions and customs; a value system with its own code of practice. It is the world of peer pressure, and it emerged when the group first formed; for the nudges and winks, the disapproving frowns and the laconic quips of his classmates will determine how, when or indeed if, a child will share a response with his teacher. The extent to which he will interact with those around him is inextricably linked to the classroom culture in which he finds himself – and, most importantly, the role that he has been given within the group. As Jackson (1994) recognises:

Learning to live in a classroom involves, among other things, learning to live in a crowd. Most of the things done in school are done with others, or at least in the presence of others, and this fact has profound implications for determining the quality of a student's life. (1994: 118)

Before responding to a teacher's question, before sharing an anecdote or expressing a view within a group discussion, and especially before asking for assistance, pupils will invariably stop and check their intentions against the group code, asking, 'Will what I am about to say be acceptable to the group, and if so, would someone like me be allowed to say it? Is it in my script?'

Labov (cited in Wood, 1988) recognises that the way in which children talk, and what they do or do not say to each other, is fundamentally affected by the social and institutional context in which they are observed. The school environment, and the group dynamics that exist within it, sets boundaries, regulating social interaction and sustaining a self-fulfilling prophecy that sees confident children receiving air time and quiet children becoming inaudible – and strategies designed to buck the trend can often prove to be counter productive.

The phrase, 'Emma, what do you think about this?' may be an enticing invitation to take the floor for some, but it can bring moments of acute embarrassment and awkwardness for others. Whether such an invitation is readily accepted or not is dependent upon how Emma is regarded in the group (or how she thinks she is regarded). As Barnes (1992) suggests, how we talk is greatly influenced by the immediate context in which we find ourselves. In this sense, 'context' is not just the matter of the physical situation but rather of how we perceive the identity and purposes of the other persons present, how we interpret whatever activities are currently being carried out, and our own place in them.

Asking Emma directly to answer a question in class simply because she has remained quiet all lesson is not enough. If Emma lacks confidence, it is because she lacks the certainty that her views will be listened to and valued within the group, especially if they are different to those of her friends. If she is 'in a shell' at all then it is, in part, the fault of the whole group for allowing her to disappear into it – and they must help her to climb out – because the social and linguistic benefits of adopting a more participatory stance outweigh the risks of 'saying the wrong thing'. In other words, it pays to join in. As Bruner (1990) identifies, language is acquired not in the role of spectator but through use. Being 'exposed' to a flow of language is not nearly so important as using it in the midst of 'doing'. The child is not learning simply what to say but how, where, to whom, and under what circumstances.

In the same way, knowledge of citizenship is acquired most effectively through active participation – it needs to be lived. As Jerome, Hayward and Young (2003) put it:

pupils learn democracy through experiencing democracy, they learn responsibility through being responsible; and they learn to participate through participating. (2003: 230).

Paradoxically, lessons in tolerance and empathy can only be truly learned when class members are tolerant enough to listen to one another. In other words, a culture of listening, valuing and responding sensitively to others' views needs to be re-established in the classroom before opinions can be expressed, and collaborative learning can begin. We must promote active 'pupilship' as a model for citizenship.

An Equitable Discourse

This book seeks to re-establish a level playing field upon which all group members may be encouraged to exchange ideas within a climate of positive support and interest. Talking together, and by that I mean listening and responding to one another's views, is the most productive occupation in which children can engage at school. The pooling of ideas and the solving of problems through negotiation and collaboration not only brings a sense of unity and cohesion to a group, it also aids the language development and personal and social growth of every individual within it. The distance between pupils' existing knowledge and their potential for learning more – known as the 'zone of proximal development' (Vygotsky, 1978) – can be bridged through verbal interaction with adults or with more able peers. In this way spoken language plays a central role in the 'scaffolding' of knowledge (Bruner).

When pupils share knowledge in this way they are sharing something of themselves and as a result, the relationship between the individual and the group will change: the individual's confidence and trust will increase and the degree of tolerance, empathy and respect within the group will rise as its members learn more about one another. In this sense oral language 'brings the self to others' (Corson, 1988), confronting learners with viewpoints that are different to their own and helping them to see that for some problems, there may be more than one solution. This is active citizenship at work.

The importance of verbal interaction is reflected in the non-statutory guidelines for PSHE and Citizenship at Key Stage 2 and the Programme of Study for Citizenship at Key Stage 3. For example, pupils are expected to be able to:

- take part in simple discussions and debates on topical issues that affect themselves and others

- talk and write about their opinions explaining their views

- ask and respond to questions and listen to the views of others

- use their imagination to consider other people's experiences and be able to think about, express and explain views that are not their own

- negotiate, decide and take part responsibly in both school and community based activities

- reflect on the process of participating.

DfEE, QCA (1999)

Similarly the value and importance of oral communication is reflected in the programmes of study for every core and foundation subject in the National Curriculum. Not only is there a discrete attainment target devoted to Speaking and Listening in the English Programme of Study, but in every subject references are made to the consolidation and sharing of knowledge through verbal communication. For example, pupils must be taught to 'identify the gist of an account', to 'ask relevant questions' and to 'respond to others appropriately'.

In Citizenship especially, emphasis is often placed on group discussion, with the pupils being encouraged to debate issues, wrestle with moral dilemmas and share ideas in response to a given topic.

So talk is unquestionably a useful teaching and learning tool in today's classroom; but we must recognise that talk is only useful when all pupils enjoy equal access to the discourse of the class. The reality is often very different: reluctant talkers won't talk at all if they feel there are too many reluctant listeners in the room, and no matter how much a conversation is teacher-led, the hierarchical system of communication that emerged from the melting pot during those first few days of the group's inception, will ensure that pupils' responses are measured and checked against the script they have been given. Their verbal contributions will be influenced by the role they play within the group. As for Citizenship, where we are primarily concerned with encouraging pupils to participate in society as active citizens, perpetuating the inequalities of the class dynamic in this way is far from useful: it can even be counterproductive.

If we are serious about empowering children to speak and so exploit properly the learning potential of an equitable classroom discourse, we must establish a climate that welcomes and respects contributions from every child. The hierarchy that has emerged within the sub-culture of peer pressure must be addressed and the group dynamics re-built.

Rebuilding Group Dynamics

If the social interaction between pupils in school is to be used as a model for the way in which citizens interact in society, then it needs to be positive and fair. For the classroom to function properly as a public forum, an atmosphere needs to be created in which all pupils feel they have something to contribute and can express themselves freely (Huddleston and Rowe, 2003). The children must be given the opportunity to practise articulating their views and responding to the views of others in an appropriate way. Just as language development requires a context that brings meaning and purpose to the words we use, so children's social and personal development require a context – a shared imagined experience in which views can be exchanged and explored within the relative safety of a role-play.

The sensitivity to other people's views that is required in the Citizenship curriculum may be built when students try out different roles, including those that contradict their own perspectives. Learning to develop empathy is the result (Wales and Clarke, 2005). Within a fictional scenario conflicting views may be assigned to different characters, thus encouraging the participants to practise tolerating and empathising with others. As the Programme of Study for Citizenship demands:

Pupils should be taught to use their imagination to consider other people's experiences and be able to think about, express and explain views that are not their own (1999: 14: 3a).

Such contexts and scenarios can bring a sense of meaning and purpose to classroom discourse. Fictitious roles may be distributed within the group in such a way that re-organises the group dynamic, enabling pupils to move away from the positions in which they have become entrenched.

First, however, we must recognise that for cohesion and synergy to exist in any group, whether it be in a fictional context or not, there must be a vision of how individual members would like the group to be. From this, certain truths or core values can be established. Then a set of rules or group pledges will serve as the building blocks for the construction and preservation of the group model. Once these concepts have been established, then positive relationships can be built and the business of collaborative learning can take place; the children can move from enforced 'pupilship' to informed Citizenship.

Creating a Vision Statement

When people come together to form a group, whether involuntarily as in the formation of a school class, or voluntarily as members of a club, there will inevitably be a disparate range of personalities, talents and skills abounding, and a whole spectrum of intentions depending upon the vested interests of the individuals within it. In other words, the relationship an individual enjoys with a group is defined by two factors: her own aspirations and needs, and the broader welfare of the group. Though there may be a conflict of interests in certain circumstances, there will usually be an agreement that there needs to exist a general level of acceptance between members and this will override the negative feelings between some (Dornyei & Murphey, 2003).

In a classroom situation, the vision statement will relate to the type of learning experience the children want to enjoy together. The sense of injustice that is often so finely tuned in many children, will no doubt enable them to articulate what the group should be like. Such a vision need not be a complex and protracted one:

We would like our group experience to be a happy and productive one, in which everyone is encouraged to share ideas and no one is excluded.

Implicit in such a vision are certain values, which are shared by the individual members of the group, and, once identified, these will form the basis of the classroom rules, or pledges.

Re-establishing Group Values

Schools are complex places precisely because they must accommodate a range of different value systems corresponding to the diverse cultures, races and social backgrounds of their pupils. As Furlong (1993) recognises, schools traditionally value certain sorts of knowledge (enshrined in the curriculum), notions of good behaviour (codified in the school and classroom rules) and aspirations for certain futures (exemplified in careers advice). The fact that pupils are not 'made' at school, but at home, in a family culture with its own value systems, indicates why for many, school values can be as divisive as they are unifying.

Yet some sort of consensus is needed for a group or class to function and for its members to interact positively and productively. If a group is to be successful at all – for its members to feel valued and actively involved – it is important that certain 'truths' which underpin positive interaction are recognized: factors that demonstrably make better cohesion in a room of children. There is something of a dichotomy here: for pupils to work hard in school they need to feel some element of control. If a pupil believes that succeeding at school depends upon her own actions she will be much more likely to attend to school tasks and concentrate on her own work than if she believes that success depends upon external factors that are outside her control (Howe, 1993). The teacher must therefore balance the need to empower individuals (in order to avoid the opportunity for inaction through a dependency on other group members) with the need to promote the benefits of pulling together. In the same way that a group's values must not obstruct the different value systems of individuals' cultural backgrounds, so a group's work ethic must not diminish or devalue the individual contributions and responsibilities of its members. Tolerance of one another's ethnic and cultural differences, empathy with one another's viewpoints and recognition of the contributions of individuals need not undermine cooperation and cohesion.

Group values, then, need to recognise and celebrate diversity, and foster tolerance, empathy and cooperation. They are the reference point around which group members may orientate their behaviour, rather than their cultural beliefs and career aspirations necessarily, revisiting the values when they feel infringements have occurred and cooperation and cohesion have broken down. Focusing on the question of group interaction, a discussion needs to take place in which pupils may articulate what they value – what they regard as the essential ingredients for a positive and productive group. It is a good idea to preface the agreed values with the words, 'We agree that...'

For example:

We agree that...

- Everyone has a voice that should be heard.

- Every idea deserves consideration.

- An open mind is often better than a strong one.

- Diversity, when tolerated, is a strength.

- No-one knows everything but together we know a lot.

- Pulling together is better than pulling apart.

Once a set of group values has been established, they need to be upheld – through the regulating and constant checking of group members' behaviour. A set of classroom rules, referred to here as 'group pledges' needs to be written to create and maintain the learning experience described in the vision statement. The term 'pledges' implies a promise to do something or act in a particular way and this is a positive place to begin, rather than to produce a list of actions that are prohibited.

Making Pledges

Exploring and short-listing group pledges to be included in a class list is in itself a worthwhile activity. The process of discussion, explaining, justifying and revising suggestions for how to behave helps to generate understanding and a positive attitude towards rules (Docking, 1996). Beginning with the shared vision, group members should remind themselves of the long-term goal in terms of group experience and then revisit the core values implied in such a vision. The group then needs to consider how to convert these into positive pledges to behave in such a way that does not infringe upon these agreed values.

For example:

Core Value: Everyone has a voice that should be heard.

Pledge: We agree to give each other time to speak.

Core Value: Every idea deserves consideration.

Pledge:	We promise to listen to each other's ideas and respond in a positive way.

Core value:	An open mind is often better than a strong one.
Pledge:	We shall try to give new ideas a chance.

Core value:	Diversity is our strength.
Pledge:	We shall always respect the differences in others.

Core value:	No one knows everything but together we know a lot.
Pledge:	We shall try, at all times, to learn from one another.

Core Value:	Pulling together is better than pulling apart.
Pledge:	We shall use our talents and strengths to achieve success together.

(Please note that the above examples feature as posters on the accompanying CD ROM and are referred to in the preliminary Lesson 2).

How to Use the Materials

The lesson plans offered in this book are divided into individual units – three for each year group in upper Key Stage 2 (ages 9 to 10) and Key Stage 3 (ages 11 to 14). These are preceded by a set of preliminary lessons that introduce the pupils to the important stages of writing a vision statement, establishing core values and making class pledges.

These preliminary lessons can be used with any year group and should precede the three individual units provided in each year.

In each unit, the class is given a scenario, a list of characters and a dispute to be resolved. In each case, there will be controversy, debate and, with luck, compromise. Each pupil will have his or her say.

The class should be separated into groups to complete the tasks. The suggested size of group, for ease of management, is approximately six pupils, though there are enough different character cards to have up to ten pupils in each group.

No-one will be excluded and, perhaps most importantly, the role each pupil will play in the group will be predetermined by the teacher and will not, as far as is practicable, be a mirror image of their 'usual role' in the class. The children will be freed from the entrenchment they may be experiencing in the aforementioned sub-culture of the class.

Each unit comprises three sections:

- lesson plans 1-4
- follow-up activities
- curriculum overview.

In each unit Context Builder Cards establish the context and scenario for the work that follows. Character Cards are then used to distribute roles among the pupils. Each of these cards are included within the body of the lesson plans, for ease of reading, while photocopiable versions are also included at the end of each unit.

The photocopiable sheets are marked with the symbol:

Context and Scenario (Context Builder Cards)

Progression is built in to the programme of units, in subject content and complexity of scenario, reflecting children's gradual maturation as they move from a predominantly egocentric view of the world towards a more participatory and empathetic one. Through a series of case studies the children are encouraged to see that they have a role and a responsibility not only as a member of their school, but as a resident in their local community and a citizen of their country and though the focus may widen as the contexts shift from local to national level, the need for positive social interaction built on tolerance, empathy and cooperation remains; the vision and core values are just as applicable throughout, and the pledges need to be adhered to. The central task in each unit is to work together to accommodate conflicting views and find a way through to a compromise. In this way the children are practising good citizenship.

The scenarios presented offer opportunities for group/whole class discussions and debates. Though the situational contexts differ, the brief is always the same: to find cohesion in difficult circumstances by resolving differences and exploring alternatives; to listen carefully to others' views and to identify and solve disputes through positive discourse – reaching a consensus through compromise. In this regard, it is important to revisit and reinforce the vision, core values and group pledges established in the preliminary lessons.

To ensure effective and meaningful participation by all pupils, and to make each role-playing session more enjoyable for all, it is important to spend time building the context in the minds of the children. For this purpose, each unit begins with a Context Builder Card that should be read out to the class. This contains an easy to follow summary of the context and a detailed explanation of the scenario. Also on each Context Builder Card is a brief glossary of terms, defining any words that may be new to the children.

Distributing Roles (Character Cards)

Each unit features different Character Cards and these are divided into two categories: characters 'for' and characters 'against' the controversial plan or scheme that is being proposed in the scenario. In discussion groups, the pupils participate 'in role', sharing views and listening to the opposing views of others.

After the context and scenario have been read out and discussed (in a preliminary circle meeting – see Lesson 1 in each unit), the children are divided into groups and given specific roles. Each character has his or her own Character Profile – a short description of the person's viewpoint (why he or she has a vested interest in the decision-making process). Again, these are included in the body of the lesson plans for ease of reading, with full photocopiable versions at the end of each unit. Each pupil must study her own character's profile carefully and become familiar with her view of the scenario, the object being that every character will have the opportunity to share her own views in the group discussion initially, and then in a general meeting that takes place later in the unit.

The purpose of the Character Profile – and the central tenet of the group activity – is to highlight how large-scale decisions directly affect the lives of individual members within a community and as such everyone has a voice that needs to be heard. For a compromise to be ultimately reached, group members will need to take time to listen to one another, and empathise with others' viewpoints. The children's listening skills can be assessed carefully by using the Character Record Sheets (appearing at the end of each unit), on to which they must record the names of the other group members, their roles and their viewpoints in relation to the controversial plan of action, during the initial group meetings in Lesson 2.

Pupils are welcome to explore ways of 'getting into' their part, although the quality of a child's acting is irrelevant; the important thing is that they express the views written on their Character Profiles in the group forum. Articulacy and persuasiveness are useful, but so too are listening skills: equitable compromise comes from sharing and hearing ideas.

Lesson Plans

The four lesson plans in each unit are designed to progress the scenario further, deepening pupils' interest and engagement and providing the opportunity for meaningful, context-based writing tasks. The latter may well form part of a homework assignment, or if time permits, separate literacy lessons may be introduced, in which the class may focus in more detail upon the language features of particular National Literacy Strategy (NLS) text-types relating to scenarios (for example, persuasive letters, speeches or diaries).

Lesson 1 begins with a circle meeting, in which the context is built and the scenario is introduced. Terms and phrases specific to the context are clarified in this initial session. Possible viewpoints are explored and potential conflicts identified, before the Character Cards and profiles are introduced (giving pupils the chance to hypothesise and explore how the proposed plans may impact on the lives of individuals). Then, once the children have had the chance to consider for themselves who might be involved in such a scenario, the Character Cards are read out. The pupils are put into groups (four to six pupils are recommended, but a maximum of ten is possible). Each group member is given a different role – half the group will be 'for' and half will be 'against' the proposed plan (a range of detailed Character Profiles will also help the pupils explore their character's viewpoint. Before the next lesson, the children will be encouraged to think about how they might express the views of their character in a group meeting (which will take place in Lesson 2).

Lesson 2 begins with a re-building of the context and a reminder of the scenario. A brief circle meeting will re-establish the importance of positive and equitable interaction – by revisiting the vision, core values and group pledges of the preliminary lessons. Pupils then return to their groups (established in Lesson 1) and begin sharing their views. The children are encouraged to complete a Character Record Sheet (a photocopiable version appears at the end of each unit), onto which they must record summaries of the viewpoints of the other members on their group, to show they have been listening. These record sheets are then collected in and marked by the teacher to assess listening skills. Once every group member has had the opportunity to share their views (and everyone else has recorded a summary of them next to the character's name and role on the character record sheet, Lesson 2 finishes with a plenary session in which the children are encouraged to share feedback, not on their specific viewpoints in role, but rather on the process of listening to and recording the views of others (see actual lesson plans for further guidance on this).

Intermediate Task

Between Lessons 2 and 3 there are opportunities for extended writing tasks, with the children producing a piece of persuasive text specifically related to each case study – this may be a formal letter to an MP, a statement or a propaganda leaflet, in which a particular viewpoint is conveyed. The texts can be referred to in the following lesson, being used as notes for the speakers or formally read aloud. Teachers may wish to display the children's work after the unit has been completed.

Lesson 3 opens with another group session, but this time with the children who are playing the same characters across the different original groups coming together to compare notes and consolidate and strengthen their cases. These support groups will elect a spokesperson (a different one each time) who will present the viewpoint on behalf of the support group in the whole class 'public' meeting that then follows. During this meeting, chaired by the teacher, the ten spokespersons (five for and five against the proposed plan – taken from the recommended characters on the Character Cards, marked 'For and 'Against' but it will depend on the number who are in the each group) will present their cases formally. Open questions from the floor then follow, during which time other pupils may have the chance to speak within this larger forum.

In this important third session, the notion of a compromise needs to be introduced, through the presentation of a range of options offered by the chairperson (suggestions for these options are offered in each case study). The central question the pupils must ask themselves is: If I cannot have exactly what I want, what would the next best thing be? Which of the options is the most acceptable or least inconvenient to me? Here, of course, the nature of reaching decisions democratically is central to the process, with a final vote highlighting where a consensus may lie.

Lesson 4 closes the case study with a class discussion on the specific scenario and solution concerned, and then more general comments on the democratic process as it unfolded. Specific questions are offered each time for the teacher to use to guide the discussion. The original vision, core values and group pledges of the preliminary lessons will serve as the reference points against which the success of each resolution may be judged.

Follow-up Activities

The follow-up activities for each unit offer further opportunities for cross-curricular work, within each particular role-play theme, and some will lend themselves to certain foundation subjects more than others. The Planning Application unit in Year 6 for example could, if time permitted, inspire a local history topic or a geography study of a UK locality, looking at how people can improve or damage the environment, or a piece of fieldwork looking at the suitability of a local site for a factory or supermarket.

Curriculum Overview

The Curriculum Overview profiles the specific attainment targets covered in the lessons and follow-up activities. This is not a definitive list, there are many more opportunities for learning across the Key Stage 2 and 3 curriculums, should you wish to plan for more. The references featured refer to the specific programmes of study in the National Curriculum for Key Stages 2 and 3. Also featured in the overview are the various NLS text types that could be incorporated into the writing aspect of each unit.

Preliminary Lessons

Lesson 1: Writing a Vision Statement

Hold a class discussion to introduce the concept of a vision statement (for example, a sentence or two that describes the kind of group that individual members would wish to be a part of, one which fosters individual talents and addresses individual needs). It is important that the pupils understand from the outset that a shared vision is important, and that it must be agreed upon by all.

Questions such as: 'What sort of group do I want to be a part of?' and, 'How do I want to be treated by others?' are integral to this process and they need to be raised in this initial plenary session.

Divide the children up into groups of about five or six. Explain to each group the task: to decide on the type of learning experience they would all like to enjoy in class and then to shape this vision into a sentence or two.

Experience tells us that children may be quick to point out the sort of experience they do not want – shouting out, pupils not listening to each other properly, distractions in class – but for this lesson, they need to consider what kind of experience they do want. You may need to start them off with an example:

We would like our group experience to be a happy and productive one, in which everyone is encouraged to share ideas and no-one is excluded.

The following questions may help you to guide the group discussions as you move around the room, monitoring progress (a photocopiable version appears at the end of this unit, labelled Sheet 1):

- When do we enjoy group work?
- Why are some groups more successful than others?
- When do we feel frustrated in group work? What goes wrong?
- Can working together in a group actually achieve something?
- What are the obstacles that prevent groups from fulfilling tasks?
- Can I see a difference between my own individual needs and the needs of the group as a whole? Which are more important?

Once each group has had a chance to debate these issues and, hopefully, to find answers to some of these difficult questions, they will need to shape their ideas into an actual statement, a positive view of working together. This will become the vision statement – the model that will guide and inform all future group interaction, so that the children can strive for this kind of experience. When behaviour breaks down and relations are strained, it will be because someone has lost the vision of what the group should be like and consequently they are spoiling the experience for the others.

Return together for a class plenary and share vision statements. Try, if you can, to identify common themes in each vision statement and work towards establishing a class vision statement. Record this final statement in a prominent place where pupils may refer back to it. You may wish to invite the children to design their own posters incorporating the vision statement.

Finally, explain to the class that when they were deciding on a vision statement earlier, they were in fact sharing what they value in class – the standards which they hold to be important in order for them to get along. These values are the subject of Preliminary Lesson 2.

Lesson 2: Establishing Group Values

Initiate a class discussion in which you introduce the verb to value and the noun values. Invite definitions for each word. You may wish to then clarify using the following Oxford dictionary definitions:

value *v.* to consider to be important or beneficial.

value(s) *n.* principles or standards of behaviour.

Consider what sort of things are traditionally valued within a school environment. Some examples to start off with are: knowledge, good behaviour, diligence, advancement, career progression.

Move on to considering how people's own different backgrounds (ethnicity, nationality, faith, family, social background and so on) may lead to them to value different things to others in the class – or perhaps value the same things more or less highly. For example, pupils of some religious faiths may value strict adherence to certain teachings and this will shape the way they live and work. Some children from different social backgrounds may value hard work and getting a job more than taking time to reflect, to travel and to explore different creative and cultural pursuits (because necessity dictates that they earn an income). Some may be brought up to become team players others may be influenced into pursuing their own goals only, and to look after themselves. When struck in the playground, some will be taught to strike back, others to show restraint.

Divide the class into groups. Working together, can the children think of other value systems and beliefs that may be specific to individuals? What are the aspects of daily life in which different values might become apparent? Where might we see different customs in action? You may wish to use the following examples (also included at the end of this preliminary unit, labelled Sheet 2):

work: some people will not work on a Sunday, for others Saturday is the day of rest

home: some people like to live in a shared community, for others, one's home is one's castle

eating and drinking: many people adhere to a strict regime of what they may or may not eat or drink, according to their faith; others follow vegetarian diets

church: there are many different forms of worship – some involve frequent trips to a place of collective worship, others involve silent, individual contemplation

healthcare: some rate herbal medicine very highly; others have strict guidelines as to what they may or may not have done in hospital, according to their faith

marriage: for some, marriages are arranged by a person's elders; for others getting married is not considered necessary for a loving relationship to flourish

clothing: some people must cover their bodies entirely in public; others don't wear any clothes at all!

You may wish for the children to consider additional examples for each of the above sections – and to think of other categories and examples too. Ask the children to make notes of their findings so that they can report back to the class in the following plenary.

After a few minutes, return together as a class and share feedback. Once you have recorded the different sorts of values and customs on the board (perhaps in a Mind Map (TM), with the title 'What do we value?' in the middle), you will need to move on to considering how the value system of a school or class needs to take into account all these disparate wants, needs and customs and to find a way through to working together.

It is in a class or group situation that the children spend most of their waking hours – so what should the group value in order for everyone to get along, and do something constructive? The group members will differ in many ways, but are there certain principles, or 'truths', that will not conflict with individuals' own personal values and will allow cooperation and cohesion? This is the key challenge for the children – to identify the basic principles that lead to good group interaction.

Divide the children into their groups once more. The task is to come up with a set of values, or principles, that everyone in the group can agree to. It is important to remind the children here of the vision statement from Lesson 1. Their task now is to consider what they need to value in order to turn this vision into a reality.

Explain to the children that they will need to begin their group values with the phrase, 'We agree that...' The following are some examples of model group values for you to use to get the children started. You may wish to refer only to one or two before the children have a go for themselves, or to distribute copies of the values, (enclosed at the end of this preliminary unit, labelled Sheet 3) to go through together first.

We agree that:

- Everyone has a voice that should be heard.
- Every idea deserves consideration.
- An open mind is often better than a strong one.
- Diversity, when tolerated, is a strength.
- No-one knows everything but together we know a lot.
- Pulling together is better than pulling apart.

Come together once again for a final plenary. Invite a spokesperson from each group to present their values to the class. If they have not already surfaced in one form or another, you may wish to revisit the above list of model values (Sheet 3), or to add some of your own.

You will need to agree on a set number of values for the class (six or seven is manageable) and then display these in a prominent place. Explain to the pupils that these values need to be remembered – the children need to promise or pledge to respect the values so that the sort of group wished for in the vision statement is created and maintained. In the final preliminary lesson the children will be considering just what those pledges should be.

Lesson 3: Making Pledges

Begin this final preliminary lesson with a class discussion in which you revisit the shared vision statement of Preliminary Lesson 1 and the agreed values established in Preliminary Lesson 2. Remind the pupils that in order to achieve, and sustain, the ideal group experience, it is important that everyone agrees to make certain promises – they must pledge to behave in such a way that respects and upholds the values that are important to them. Knowing what works in a group – that is, understanding the values that underpin positive interaction – and actually making it work everyday are very different things. In other words, the children may have been successful so far in agreeing on a vision and on a set of 'truths' that they hold to be important, but what they must do now is turn the words into actions.

Read out, in turn, each of the agreed values from Lesson 2. Starting with the first, (here we shall use the example of 'Everyone has a voice that should be heard'), invite the children to think of a class rule or 'pledge' that could accompany this value, to make sure that everyone's voice is actually heard. A possible pledge might be:

We agree to give each other time to speak.

Divide the class into groups (four to six is ideal). Explain the following group task to be completed: Each group must work together to find a pledge for each of the values established in Lesson 2. The pledges need to be a similarly concise sentence, easy to comprehend and linked closely to the theme of each value.

You may wish to use the following examples either at the beginning, if pupils are struggling, or in the final plenary. A photocopiable version is enclosed at the end of this unit, labelled Sheet 4.

Core Value:	Everyone has a voice that should be heard.
Pledge:	We agree to give each other time to speak.
Core Value:	Every idea deserves consideration.
Pledge:	We promise to listen to each other's ideas and respond in a positive way.
Core value:	An open mind is often better than a strong one.
Pledge:	We shall try to give new ideas a chance.
Core value:	Diversity is our strength.
Pledge:	We shall always respect the differences in others.
Core value:	No one knows everything but together we know a lot.
Pledge:	We shall try, at all times, to learn from one another.
Core Value:	Pulling together is better than pulling apart.
Pledge:	We shall use our talents and strengths to achieve success together.

The groups will need to present their ideas on a large A3 sheet, using a marker pen. Each value will be written out neatly, and below it will be the class pledge (as in the examples on Sheet 4). Alternatively you may wish for the groups to present their work using interactive media.

Return together for a final plenary. Invite an elected spokesperson from each group to present their values and pledges, and discuss how they reached them.

An interesting exercise here is to investigate whether, during this group task, the pupils managed to keep to the values and pledges they were making. Did everyone have a turn to speak, for example? Did group members respect others' ideas?

Close by reminding the children that the whole process of writing a vision statement, establishing group values and making pledges was in order to establish tolerance, empathy and cooperation in the working environment.

The following units will involve some challenging scenarios. There will be some very different views aired. There will be controversy, debate and disagreement. But if the pupils learn to tolerate each other's differences, empathise with each other's viewpoints and cooperate throughout, they will find solutions.

This is what citizenship is about. Good luck.

When do we enjoy group work?

When do we feel frustrated in group work? What goes wrong?

What are the obstacles that prevent groups from fulfilling tasks?

Why are some groups more successful than others?

Can working together in a group actually achieve something?

Can we see a difference between my own individual needs and the needs of the group as a whole? Which are more important?

Work:

Some people will not work on a Sunday, for others Saturday is the day of rest.

Eating and drinking:

Many people adhere to a strict regime of what they may or may not eat or drink, according to their faith; others follow vegetarian diets.

Church:

There are many different forms of worship – some involve frequent trips to a place of collective worship, others involve silent, individual contemplation.

Healthcare:

Some rate herbal medicine very highly; others have strict guidelines as to what they may or may not have done in hospital, according to their faith.

Marriage:

For some, marriages are arranged by a person's elders; for others getting married is not considered necessary for a loving relationship to flourish.

Clothing:

Some people must cover their bodies entirely in public; others don't wear any clothes at all!

We agree that:

- Everyone has a voice that should be heard.

- Every idea deserves consideration.

- An open mind is often better than a strong one.

- Diversity, when tolerated, is a strength.

- No-one knows everything but together we know a lot.

- Pulling together is better than pulling apart.

Core Value: Everyone has a voice that should be heard.

Pledge: We agree to give each other time to speak.

Core Value: Every idea deserves consideration.

Pledge: We promise to listen to each other's ideas and respond in a positive way.

Core value: An open mind is often better than a strong one.

Pledge: We shall try to give new ideas a chance.

Core value: Diversity, when tolerated, is a strength.

Pledge: We shall always respect the differences in others.

Core value: No one knows everything but together we know a lot.

Pledge: We shall try, at all times, to learn from one another.

Core Value: Pulling together is better than pulling apart.

Pledge: We shall use our talents and strengths to achieve success.

Pupil Name:

Character Role:

Views:

Pupil Name:

Character Role:

Views:

Pupil Name:

Character Role:

Views:

Pupil Name:

Character Role:

Views:

Pupil Name:

Character Role:

Views:

Playground Plans

Section 1: Lesson Plans

Lesson 1

Arrange a circle meeting for the whole class. Introduce the theme for the unit by reading out the following Context Builder 1 (a photocopiable version appears at the end of this unit).

Context Builder 1	Unit 1 (Year 5)

Context	The Friends Association at Treegap Primary School has been working hard this year! A fete, a Bingo Night, two sponsored Fun-Runs and a Summer Ball have raised a grand total of £15,000 – all to be spent for the benefit of Treegap's pupils... but on what?
Scenario	The current proposal is to spend the money on a new adventure playground for the infants. However, many people in the Treegap community feel that there are more urgent, or more deserving causes within the school. It's time to hold a meeting to hear views. If the money is not spent soon, the Friends of Treegap will feel less inclined to put in the hard work again next year!
Glossary	*Friends* – An association of parents, carers, staff and governors who meet regularly to organise fundraising events and appeals on behalf of the school.

Governor – a member of a committee, or 'governing body' that is responsible for the overall management of a school and its budget. |

Elicit pupils' existing knowledge of School Friends Associations – explain and clarify any points. Discuss the idea of spending the money on a new adventure playground for Key Stage 1. Does it sound like a good idea? Who might support such a plan – who might oppose it? Can the children think of other areas and departments in a school that might need the money just as much? What else might this donation buy? Establish ways in which people who have different ideas about how the money should be spent could express their views (such as letters, telephone calls and meetings).

Initiate a discussion about the importance of respecting other people's views and responding to others' ideas sensitively and appropriately. Encourage the pupils to see the importance of finding solutions and compromises which keep the greatest number of people happy, also of the need to ensure that the Friends Association feel their hard fundraising efforts have been worthwhile and their money is both needed and welcome!

When everyone has had the chance to contribute, establish the groups for the unit. You may wish to record the names in each group for future lessons. Then read out the following Character Cards (also enclosed at the end of this unit for photocopying) and give each pupil a role to play.

Character Card: For   Unit 1 (Year 5)

The following characters are in favour of the new playground:

Recommended characters:

- Year 2 class teacher (and PSHE coordinator)
- parent of twins in Year 1
- playground supervisor
- school governor (runs an Outward Bound Centre)
- PE coordinator.

Further suggestions:

parent and leader of local Cub Pack

carer of reception pupil

grandparent of Year 2 pupil (ex-army officer)

deputy headteacher (and keen camper)

teacher and Summer Camp coordinator.

Character Card: Against   Unit 1 (Year 5)

The following characters are against the plans for a new playground:

Recommended characters:

- music coordinator
- parent of reception pupil
- school first-aid officer
- school governor (runs an IT business)
- library coordinator.

Further suggestions:

school Health and Safety Officer

general teaching assistant – Playground Supervisor

art coordinator

ex-governor and dance teacher

grandparent of Year 1 pupil (and professional musician).

Individual Character Profiles (at the end of this unit) will offer each pupil a brief summary of his or her character's viewpoint in relation to the scenario.

There are a total of ten characters available (five recommended characters from each side), though others are suggested and may be added if necessary. All pupils in each group must receive a different role – and preferably half the roles will come from Character Card: For and the other half from Character Card Against.

Explain to the pupils what is to happen next: before the next workshop (Lesson 2), the pupils must spend time developing opinions and constructing arguments in note form, on behalf of their character. Each pupil will need to come to the group prepared to defend the views of their character, persuading others in the group to see the issue from their viewpoint. During the intervening period between lessons, (this may be a day or a week, depending on your timetable), you may wish to invite children to seek your help, or the help of others, if they encounter problems in finding ideas for their own character.

Lesson 2

Begin with a circle meeting. Revisit the vision statement, core values and group pledges of the preliminary lessons. Reiterate the importance of abiding by the pledges when interacting within the group discussions that will follow.

The pupils then reform the groups from Lesson 1. Give a copy of the Character Record Sheet to every pupil (included at the end of this unit). Each group member will have a turn to share their opinions and arguments in respect of the proposed plans. Pupils will need to listen carefully to each other, noting down the names, roles and a brief two-line summary of the views of the other members in their group. The record sheets need to be collected in at the end of the lesson for the teacher to assess whether the children have been listening well and the information recorded about their fellow group members is correct (this can be checked against the Character Cards and Profiles).

At the end of the session, hold a short plenary in which children are invited to report back to the whole class NOT on their specific views and arguments, but on the process of sharing opinions – was it helpful to find others with similar views? Was there a sense of different sides forming in the group as people discovered who shared their own views and who did not? Which was easier, expressing one's own viewpoint or listening to the views of another? Did the children find themselves paying more attention to those who shared similar views to their own?

Explain to the pupils the next step in the unit – each pupil is to prepare a formal letter, addressed to the Chair of the Friends Association, in which they express their views, clearly and persuasively, on the playground plans – sharing their own thoughts on how the money should be spent.

The next workshop will be a 'public meeting' hosted by the Chairperson of the Friends Association (that is, the teacher) in which some of the letters be read out formally and then everyone will have the chance to speak or ask questions.

Lesson 3

The lesson begins with a short group session in which the pupils playing the same characters across the groups get together to share ideas and put together strong cases. They can refer to their letters for their views if they wish. Each group of 'like-characters' will need to elect a spokesperson (the teacher may need to intervene here). The elected spokesperson will be speaking at the following 'public' meeting.

Come together as a class and explain the procedure for the final 'public' meeting: there will be a table at the front of the room from which the Chair of the Friends Association (the teacher) will host the meeting. Sitting either side of the Chairperson will be the elected spokespersons (one of every character from cards For and Against (that is, five on each side). The format for the meeting can be altered to suit timings and location, but a suggested order might be:

Chairperson (that is, the teacher) opens the meeting with an explanation of the current proposal to spend the money on a new adventure playground.

- Chairperson invites each of the characters to present their viewpoints.

- Chairperson invites comments from the floor – this is an opportunity for other pupils to ask questions or express their views.

- Final vote – for this you will need to distil the different ideas into a shortlist of options. These might include:

Spend all of the money on the adventure playground

Spend all of the money on something else

Put some money to one side to begin saving for the playground, and spend the rest on something else.

Once the options have been established – all pupils vote for the one they would settle for.

It is important to remind the children of the need for a compromise here. The different characters may well have different views – and it was very important that these were properly heard. However, now it is time for action and the pupils need to consider the question:

If I cannot have exactly what I want, what would the next best thing be?

Lesson 4

This shorter session comprises of a class discussion (out of role), in which all pupils may feedback to the rest of the group their thoughts on the role-play. The meeting can be an informal discussion loosely based around the themes of tolerance, empathy and cooperation, or you may wish to lead the session using the following questions as a guide:

- Was the final decision the right one? How can we tell?

- What did the pupils find easy or hard about the process?

- Why were there so many different views at Treegap?

- What was the difference between talking and writing about their views? Which was easier?

Section 2: Follow-up Activities

Shopping list

The children imagine they have a grant of £15,000 to spend on resources for their school. What would they spend it on? Encourage the children to conduct research on the internet and in magazines to see what £15,000 could buy for the school. What does the school need? Would they spend it on one item, or on several? Ask the pupils to make a list of the items they would buy, together with a note of the prices (remember not to go over budget!).

Design projects

Divide the class into small working groups of three or four. Each group must come up with a design for the new adventure playground. After exploring different designs in rough, the children must produce a finished design on an A3 sheet, annotating it with different labels to show its special features and facilities. You may wish for the children to explore actual size, measurements and how to draw scale drawings of the equipment.

Persuasive writing

Using the chosen design for the playground (above), the children must plan and produce a manufacturer's promotional flyer for the playground – the sort that might be sent to prospective schools, advertising its features and persuading readers to purchase it.

Formal letter

The pupils imagine that they are the Chairperson of the Friends Association for Treegap Primary. They have received a large number of letters from people in the community, some in support of the plan to build a new playground, others firmly against it. Referring to the compromise that was reached in Lesson 3, the Chairperson must reply to each letter, justifying the final decision. Each pupil will reply to one of the letters written in a previous session above.

Section 3: Curriculum Overview

Curriculum Overview	National Curriculum references
PSHE and Citizenship	1a, 1c, 2a, 2e, 2f, 2h, 2j, 4a, 5a, 5c-e, 5g
English	En1: 1-7, En2: 3b-g, 5a-g, 9a, 9c En3: 1a-e, 2a, 3, 7c, 9c, 9d, 10, 12
NLS Text Types	persuasive: formal letters, leaflets, advertisements informative: annotated designs, budget notes and spending plans.
Mathematics	Ma2: 1a, 1h, 4a, 4b, Ma3: 1a, 1e, 4a
ICT	2a, 3a-b, 4a-c, 5a-b
Art and design	1a-c, 2a-c, 4a-b, 5b-d
Design and technology	1a, 1b, 1d, 2a-c,

Context Builder 1	Unit 1 (Year 5)

Context   The Friends Association at Treegap Primary School has been working
hard this year! A fete, a Bingo Night, two sponsored Fun-Runs and a Summer Ball
have raised a grand total of £15,000 – all to be spent for the benefit of Treegap's
pupils... but on what?

Scenario   The current proposal is to spend the money on a new adventure playground for
the infants. However, many people in the Treegap community feel that there are
more urgent, or more deserving causes within the school. It's time to hold a
meeting to hear views. If the money is not spent soon, the Friends of Treegap will
feel less inclined to put in the hard work again next year!

Glossary   *Friends* – An association of parents, carers, staff and governors who meet regularly
to organise fundraising events and appeals on behalf of the school.

Governor – a member of a committee, or 'governing body' that is responsible for
the overall management of a school and its budget.

Character Card: For	Unit 1 (Year 5)

The following characters are in favour of the new playground:

Recommended characters:

- Year 2 class teacher (and PSHE coordinator)
- parent of twins in Year 1
- playground supervisor
- school governor (runs an Outward Bound Centre)
- PE coordinator.

Further suggestions:

parent and leader of local Cub Pack

carer of reception pupil

grandparent of Year 2 pupil (Ex-army officer)

deputy headteacher (and keen camper)

teacher and Summer Camp coordinator.

Character Card: Against	Unit 1 (Year 5)

The following characters are against the plans for a new playground:

Recommended characters:

- music coordinator
- parent of reception pupil
- school first-aid officer
- school governor (runs an IT business)
- library coordinator.

Further suggestions:

school Health and Safety Officer

general teaching assistant – Playground Supervisor

art coordinator

ex-governor and dance teacher

grandparent of Year 1 pupil (and professional musician).

Character Profile 1: Year 2 Class teacher (and PSHE Coordinator)

You have felt for some time now that there are not enough climbing frames and slides for the younger children in the school. The pupils in your Year 2 class often say to you that there is nowhere for them to practise their climbing and swinging together. There is an assault course for the older pupils in the school, but the little ones have to make do with an empty playground and a few footballs. When you hear talk of a new adventure playground for your pupils, you think it is 'about time too'!

Character Profile 2: Parent of twins in Year 1

Your twin boys love climbing, swinging and sliding. In fact, given the opportunity they would join a cage of monkeys at the zoo if they could. If only the school had somewhere for them to 'let off steam' at playtime. Recently you have been receiving complaints from the boy's teacher that they are becoming increasingly restless in class. You feel it is simply because they don't have the chance to let off steam in the way they know best – climbing things!

Character Profile 3: Playground supervisor

Watching the boys and girls each day, as they run up and down the same patch of tarmac, leaves you feeling frustrated. You know that at other schools the younger children have swings and slides and, at one local school where your friend works, the children have an entire wooden fort in which to play their imaginary games. As a playground supervisor you see more than your fair share of arguments and disputes between the children. You feel certain that increasing the play facilities for the pupils would ease tension in the playground and end those frequent comments, 'Miss, I'm bored!'

Character Profile 4: School Governor (with an Outward Bound Centre)

As a school governor you have a special interest in the welfare of the pupils. As the manager of an outward bound centre for young people, you are particularly interested in helping children to stay fit and active. You believe that it is important for them to develop their muscles and build their confidence through climbing, swinging and other forms of physical adventure. The new playground will not just give them a bit of fun, but it will give them much needed exercise too.

Character Profile 5: PE Coordinator

Running around is all good fun, but as far as you are concerned, children need to be conquering climbing frames, swinging on ropes and building up their muscles. The adventure playground for the older pupils at the school has been a real success and so, provided it is safe for the little ones, an additional playground for the Key Stage One children would be good news as far as you are concerned. You might even use it in your P.E. lessons.

Character Profile 6: Music Coordinator

The playground plans may well be a good idea but what about the school's musical resources? You barely have enough recorders to form a group, and as for brass instruments you can only show your children pictures of trumpets and trombones! You have just ten mini-keyboards to share around classes of thirty. Fifteen thousand pounds would come in very handy and the instruments you could buy would be used by the whole school – not just the children in Key Stage 1.

Character Profile 7: Parent of Reception Pupil

You have heard the news that the Friends Association is considering purchasing a new adventure playground for the younger children at the school. Your daughter, Emily, is very accident-prone. She has fallen from swings, slipped down steps and once she suffered a particularly nasty fall from a slide. Understandably you are quite content with Emily just running around in the current playground, without being tempted by climbing frames and wooden forts. Besides, where are the cookery resources the Headteacher promised at the beginning of the year?

Character Profile 8: School Health and Safety Officer

When the first adventure playground was installed you did not share everyone's enthusiasm. Worried about the height of the slide and the potentially slippery surfaces of a rain-soaked bridge, you felt that the playground was an accident waiting to happen. Nevertheless the plans went ahead. This time, when the plans of building a similar facility for the little ones are announced, you decide enough is enough. No matter how safe the new playground may be, nothing is safer than the flat surface they currently have – after all they can't fall off the ground can they?

Character Profile 9: School Governor (with an IT business)

As a school governor and manager of a local IT business you have been emphasising for some time the importance of maintaining up to date ICT resources in the school. The current facilities were installed several years ago and they are in need of updating. You have offered to use your contacts in the business to secure a good deal for the school, in which you could provide a range of new PCs and software to raise the standard of ICT teaching across the school. The cost would be fifteen thousand pounds – the same price as the proposed adventure playground.

Character Profile 10: Library Coordinator

For some time now the Headteacher has been promising to increase the school's library budget to enable you to buy more stock. Many of the books in the library have sat on the shelves for many years, collecting dust. You feel that children will only come in and use the library's resources if you can offer them exciting new titles from a range of different genres. The non-fiction books for example are in short supply and the atlases show a world map that is barely recognisable today! A donation of fifteen thousand pounds would make a lot of young readers very happy indeed – and isn't reading more important than sitting on a swing?

Character Record Sheet

Name.....................................

Pupil name:	
Character role:	
Views:	

Pupil name:	
Character role:	
Views:	

Pupil name:	
Character role:	
Views:	

Pupil name:	
Character role:	
Views:	

Pupil name:	
Character role:	
Views:	

Mind The Bumps

Section 1: Lesson Plans

Lesson 1

Arrange a circle meeting for the whole class. Introduce the theme for the unit by reading out the following Context Builder 2 (a photocopiable version appears at the end of this unit).

Context Builder 2	Unit 2 (Year 5)
Context	Brookfield Primary is located on Brookfield Street – a long, main road with many houses and shops on it. Early morning commuters, daily delivery drivers and late night racers often disobey the speed limit for the area, turning the road into a hazardous race track. Something must be done, for the sake of the school children who have to cross the road every day.
Scenario	Plans are being drawn up for the entire road to be fitted with speed bumps – ramps that stretch across the road forcing drivers to slow down as they mount them, or risk causing damage to their vehicles. However, though everyone agrees the cars should slow down, the speed bumps do not meet universal approval.
Glossary	*Speed bump* – a rubber or asphalt ramp designed to decrease traffic speed. *Commuter* – person who travels the same journey to work every day.

Elicit pupils' existing knowledge and experience of speed limits. Do drivers always keep to them? Consider ways in which traffic speed can be slowed down and regulated. Why would traffic speed be especially important on Brookfield Street?

Move on to discussing speed bumps. Ensure pupils understand what they are – where they are used and how they slow traffic speed. Encourage the children to consider reasons why people might not favour them – are there any disadvantages to them? It is important here to make the point that the arguments against the speed bumps may not be based simply on a desire to drive fast, but on whether the ramps are the best way of slowing cars down. Note also that if we are going to argue against a plan – it is only right that we offer an alternative one.

Initiate a discussion about the importance of respecting other people's views and responding to others' ideas sensitively and appropriately. Emphasize the importance of identifying common aims – that is, to decrease traffic speed to make Brookfield Street a safer place for pedestrians. Encourage the pupils to see the importance of finding solutions and compromises that keep the greatest number of people happy – and most importantly will be abided by. In this case study of course, though some people may not favour the outcome, it is against the law to drive above the speed limit!

When everyone has had the chance to contribute, establish the groups for the unit. You may wish to record the names in each group for future lessons. Then read out the following Character Cards (photocopiable versions appear at the end of this unit), and give each pupil a role to play.

Character Card: For   Unit 2 (Year 5)

The following characters are in favour of installing speed ramps:

Recommended characters:

- parent of two school children
- parent of twins in Year I
- playground Supervisor
- school governor (runs an Outward Bound Centre)
- PE coordinator.

Further suggestions:

elderly resident

shop owner

headteacher of school

grandparent of school children

local campaigner for the environment.

Character Card: Against   Unit 2 (Year 5)

The following characters are against the plans for a new playground:

Recommended characters:

- local resident
- daily commuter
- local ambulance driver
- parent of school child
- local delivery driver.

Further suggestions:

local bus driver

fire officer

second local resident

owner of local garage

shopkeeper.

Individual Character Profiles (included at the end of this unit) will offer each pupil a brief summary of his or her character's viewpoint in relation to the scenario – that is, how and why they will be affected by the outcome.

There are a total of ten characters available (five recommended characters from each side), though others may be added if necessary. All pupils in each group must receive a different role – and preferably half the roles will come from Character Card: For and the other half from Character Card Against.

Explain to the pupils what is to happen next: before the next workshop (Lesson 2), the pupils must spend time developing opinions and constructing arguments in note form, on behalf of their character. Each pupil will need to come to the group prepared to argue for or against the installation of the speed ramps – with good reasons to support their arguments. During the intervening period between lessons, (this may be a day or a week, depending on your timetable), you may wish to invite children to seek your help, or the help of others, if they encounter problems in finding ideas for their own character.

Lesson 2

Begin with a circle meeting. Revisit the vision statement, core values and group pledges of the preliminary lessons. Reiterate the importance of abiding by the pledges when interacting within the group discussions that follow.

The pupils reform the groups from Lesson 1. Give a copy of the Character Record Sheet to every pupil. Each group member will have a turn to share their opinions and arguments in respect of the proposed plans. Pupils will need to listen carefully to each other's views, noting down the names, roles and a brief two-line summary of the views of the other members in their group. Collect in the record sheets at the end of the session – and check against the original Character Profile cards.

At the end of the session, hold a short plenary in which children are invited to report back to the whole class not on their specific views and arguments, but on the process of sharing opinions – was it helpful to find others with similar views? Was there a sense of different sides forming in the group as people discovered who shared their own views and who did not? Which was easier, expressing one's own viewpoint or listening to the views of another? Did the children find themselves paying more attention to those who shared similar views to their own?

Explain to the pupils the next step in the unit – each pupil is to prepare a letter to the local newspaper ('readers' page) in which they state their own views on the proposed traffic controlling system for Brookfield Street. The next workshop will be a 'public meeting' hosted by a representative from Brookfield Borough Council (that is the teacher) in which some of the letters be read out formally, after which everyone will have the chance to speak or ask questions.

Lesson 3

The lesson begins with a short group session in which pupils who are playing the same characters across the groups get together to share ideas and thoughts, and prepare a good case. They can refer to their letters for their views if they wish. Each group of 'like-characters' will need to elect a spokesperson (some one different from the spokesperson of Unit 1). The elected speaker will address the class at the following 'public' meeting.

Come together as a class and explain the procedure for the public meeting. There will be a table at the front of the room from which the representative from Brookfield Borough Council (the teacher) will host the meeting. Sitting either side of the Chairperson will be the elected spokespersons (one of every character from the character cards, that is, five on each side). The format for the meeting can be altered to suit timings and location, but a suggested order might be:

- Chairperson (the teacher) opens the meeting with an explanation of the current proposal to install traffic ramps (speed bumps) to Brookfield Street in order to decrease and regulate traffic speed.

- Chairperson invites each of the characters to present their viewpoints, beginning with a supporter in favour of the speed bumps, and then alternating between supporters and opposers.

- Chairperson invites comments from the floor – this is an opportunity for other pupils to ask questions or express their views.

- Final vote – for this you will need to distil the different ideas into a shortlist of options. These might include:

    1. Install speed bumps along Brookfield Street.

    2. Install speed bumps on the short stretch of road outside the school only.

    3. Explore alternative forms of speed control.

    4. Have no traffic speed controlling system installed.

Once the options have been established – all pupils vote for the one they would settle for.

It is important to remind the children that although all drivers must drive safely at all times, the traffic speed controlling system that meets the most approval will the be the one that is most obeyed!

The different characters may well have different views – and it was very important that these were properly heard. However, once the options are listed, pupils need to consider the question:

If I cannot have exactly what I want, what would the next best thing be?

Lesson 4

This shorter session comprises of a class discussion (out of role), in which all pupils may feedback to the rest of the group their thoughts on the role-play. The meeting can be an informal discussion loosely based around the themes of tolerance, empathy and cooperation, or you may wish to lead the session using the following questions as a guide:

- Was the final decision the right one? How can we tell?

- How are local issues usually debated and decided?

- How do councils listen to the residents in their town?

- Why do people write to newspapers? Can a reader's letter in a newspaper actually have any effect?

- Are there any issues in their locality that are dividing opinions?

Section 2: Follow-up Activities

Road Plans

As one of the Highways Officers at Brookfield Borough Council, you are responsible for the allocation of traffic speed control systems (including speed ramps and 'slow down' signs). Your task is to work out: how many ramps and signs are required for Brookfield Street, where they should be installed and the total cost of the job.

The facts you will need are: Brookfield Street is 1200 metres long; the cost of installing one ramp is £1350; the cost of erecting one sign is £315.00; your total budget is £16,500. Draw a scaled drawing of the road, showing how many ramps and signs you would use and where you would put them.

Persuasive Posters

Your school has been asked by Brookfield Borough Council to design some posters that can be displayed on signs along the main road, reminding drivers to slow down. You will need to make your posters visually persuasive – reminding drivers of the importance of driving with care and attention at all times. You will need to use an effective combination of visuals and catchy slogans.

Playscripts

Imagine two parents in conversation outside the school gates at Brookfield Primary. They are discussing the proposed plans for the speed ramps. One parent supports the plans, the other believes that the ramps are not safe and has real concerns about them. Write the conversation as a playscript – remember to include some stage directions to help actors and actresses to perform the piece.

Design

Divide the class into small working groups of three or four. Each group projects must come up with a design for a new type of traffic speed controlling system – along the lines of speed ramps but using a different structure. After exploring different designs in rough, the children must produce a finished design on an A3 sheet, annotating it with different labels to show its special features and facilities. You may wish for the children to explore actual size, measurements and how to draw scale drawings of the equipment.

Section 3: Curriculum Overview

Curriculum Overview	National Curriculum references
PSHE and Citizenship	1a, 1c, 2a, 2e, 2d, 2f, 4a, 5a, 5c-e, 5g
English	En1: 1-7, En2: 3f, 3g, 5b, 9a, 9c En3: 1a-e, 2a, 3, 6a, 7c, 9c, 9d, 10, 12 En3: 1a-e, 2a, 3, 6a, 7c, 9c, 9d, 10, 12
NLS Text Types	playscripts persuasive: formal letters, posters, informative: annotated designs and plans, budget notes.
Mathematics	Ma2: 1a, 1h, 4a, 4b, Ma3: 1a, 1e, 4a, Ma4: 1a-f
Geography	1d, 1e, 2e, 2g, 3e, 5a
ICT	2a, 3a-b, 4b, 5a
Art and design	1a-c, 2a, 2c, 3a, 4a-b, 5b
Design and technology	1a, 1b, 1d, 2a-c, 3a, 5b

Context Builder 2	Unit 2 (Year 5)

Context   Brookfield Primary is located on Brookfield Street – a long, main road with many houses and shops on it. Early morning commuters, daily delivery drivers and late night racers often disobey the speed limit for the area, turning the road into a hazardous race track. Something must be done, for the sake of the school children who have to cross the road every day.

Scenario   Plans are being drawn up for the entire road to be fitted with speed bumps – ramps that stretch across the road forcing drivers to slow down as they mount them, or risk causing damage to their vehicles. However, though everyone agrees the cars should slow down, the speed bumps do not meet universal approval.

Glossary   *Speed bump* – a rubber or asphalt ramp designed to decrease traffic speed.

Commuter – person who travels the same journey to work every day.

Character Card: For — Unit 2 (Year 5)

The following characters are in favour of installing speed ramps:

Recommended characters:

- parent of two school children
- parent of twins in Year 1
- playground Supervisor
- school governor (runs an Outward Bound Centre)
- PE coordinator.

Further suggestions:

elderly resident

shop owner

headteacher of school

grandparent of school children

local campaigner for the environment.

Character Card: Against — Unit 2 (Year 5)

The following characters are against the plans for a new playground:

Recommended characters:

- local resident
- daily commuter
- local ambulance driver
- parent of school child
- local delivery driver.

Further suggestions:

local bus driver

fire officer

second local resident

owner of local garage

shopkeeper.

Character Profile 1: Parent of two school children

The daily walk to school is getting more and more hazardous as commuters speed past in their cars. If ever a child ran out into the road, you are sure that some of the drivers would fail to stop in time because of the speed at which they are travelling. It is a constant worry for you, and you know a great many parents at the school who feel the same. A friend has just had speed ramps fitted on her road and early signs show that they are really working. You believe that the same should be done for Brookfield Street – and soon!

Character Profile 2: Road-crossing supervisor

Trying to find a break in the busy traffic that hurtles past, so that you can step out with your crossing sign is never easy – but with the speed that some of the drivers go, you worry that their braking systems just couldn't cope if one day they didn't see you walk out. You are sure that soon there will be a pile up, with cars driving into the back of others – and you will get the blame for making them have to stop. It is definitely time that drivers slowed down. If speed bumps work, then let's get them installed – before it's too late.

Character Profile 3: Local resident

Brookfield Street used to be quite a peaceful place to live, but nowadays with speeding commuters waking you up in the morning and late night racers turning the road into a race-track at midnight, you are feeling increasingly anxious. If you ever dare to try to cross the road, the drivers only speed up and honk their horn at you. Something must be done, and soon. If this goes on much longer, you will have no alternative but to move – and leave the house you have lived in for nearly forty years.

Character Profile 4: Local shopper

Trying to find a parking space along Brookfield Street is hard enough, but when you've got a 'wannabe' racing driving on your tail it is a very stressful occupation. If you drive at the correct speed and obey the speed limit signs, they just drive very close to your bumper, forcing you to speed up. Then, once you have parked and need to reverse back onto the road, it is like reversing onto a motorway. In your own street near by, the council have fitted speed ramps and they certainly seem to be working. It is time they did the same for Brookfield Street.

Character Profile 5: Police officer

Brookfield Street is known locally as the 'race track'. If you were to chase and confront every motorist that broke the speed limit on that road, you would not be able to patrol anywhere else in the borough. You must have a traffic speed control system fitted soon so that you can devote your time to fighting other forms of crime as well. Speed ramps have proven to be very successful in neighbouring roads, where you have seen a definite decline in motoring offences recently.

Character Profile 6: Local resident

You share the view that some motorists are driving too fast. At night time especially the sound of speeding cars keeps you awake, but you have your doubts whether speed ramps are the answer. You had speed ramps where you lived previously and the noise of the cars going over the ramps and then accelerating in between them disturbed you even more. You feel sure that the most effective solution is to use speed cameras.

Character Profile 7: Daily commuter

It is bad enough sitting in long queues of traffic on the busy road every morning, but to have to wait while everyone slowly crawls over each speed bump is just too much! With so many cars driving down Brookfield Street, what chance do motorists have to go fast anyway?

Character Profile 8: Local ambulance driver

Travelling to and from emergencies is difficult enough in the busy built up area of Brookfield Street, with its side roads, driveways and roadside parking, but to have to slow down for speed ramps too will certainly add precious seconds to your journeys. You have seen enough road accidents to know that motorists need to slow down, but for the emergency services, speed ramps are nothing but a curse.

Character Profile 9: Parent of school child

As the parent of a pupil at Brookfield Primary, you welcome plans to reduce the speed of motorists that pass the school gates every morning. However, you are very wary of the speed ramps. If hit at speed, they can cause cars to veer off to the left or right, and with so many school children walking down the pavements just a few inches away, they are just not safe. You have also seen many drivers zigzag their way around speed bumps, driving even closer to the pavement. You wish the drivers would slow down – but if they are going to drive fast, it is better they did so in a straight line than over obstacles.

Character Profile 10: Local delivery driver

You travel to and from the shops at Brookfield many times a day, often with a fully laden load. Your van is only a small one and there have been several occasions when you have clipped your exhaust pipe on those wretched bumps in neighbouring streets. Now they plan to fit the same for this high street. You can see the garage bills mounting up already. Slowing the cars down is one thing – breaking their exhausts is quite another. There must be a better way.

Character Record Sheet   Name...................................

Pupil name:
Character role:
Views:

Pupil name:
Character role:
Views:

Pupil name:
Character role:
Views:

Pupil name:
Character role:
Views:

Pupil name:
Character role:
Views:

Bike Ride, Anyone?

Section 1: Lesson Plans

Lesson 1

Arrange a circle meeting for the whole class. Introduce the theme for the unit by reading out the following Context Builder 3 (a photocopiable version appears at the end of this unit).

Context Builder 3	Unit 3 (Year 5)
Context	The year is 2015 and the country is in crisis: the problem – cars. The last ten years have seen such a rise in the number of vehicles on our roads, new highways are having to be built, existing roads are being widened and fuel emissions continue to fog the skies. It is time for action.
Scenario	The government is proposing to bring in a new bill, The Vehicle Limitation Act, which will limit the number of cars to one per family (excluding works vehicles). Good prices will be paid for surplus cars currently owned, and these will be sold off to other countries with fewer cars. Public transport will be improved and the number of bicycle lanes will be increased. All good news for the environment, but not everyone is happy....
Glossary	*Bill* – a draft form of an Act of Parliament, or law.
	Fuel emissions – the gases that enter the atmosphere from a car's exhaust.

Elicit pupils' initial thoughts about traffic congestion and the harmful effects of fuel emissions. Consider how the environment may be effected by the continued construction of roads to accommodate so many vehicles.

Then consider just why people need so many cars. Talk about the notion of two parents working (where years ago perhaps only one may have gone out to work). Talk about the increase in sports and leisure centres, activity centres and many other similar places that require parents to make journeys (where years ago the children may have played in the street for amusement). Consider the nation's obsession with cars – for fun, for status etc.

Move on to discussing the proposed plan to bring in the Vehicle Limitation Act. Explain that this bill would limit the number of vehicles per family to one, excluding vehicles that are proven to be used in work-related activity (in other words a family may have one privately used vehicle and a delivery van for father's work). Consider who might agree with this bill, and who might oppose it.

Initiate a discussion about the importance of respecting other people's views and responding to others' ideas sensitively and appropriately. Emphasize the importance of identifying common aims, that is to clean up the environment, protect wildlife etc., but are there other solutions?

When everyone has had the chance to contribute, establish the groups for the unit. You may wish to record the names in each group for future lessons. Then read out the following Character Cards, (also enclosed at the end of the unit, for photocopying), and give each pupil a role to play.

Character Card: For   Unit 3 (Year 5)

The following characters are in favour of The Vehicle Limitation Act:

Recommended characters:

- wildlife campaigner
- cyclist
- member of Greenpeace
- parent with young children
- family doctor (GP).

Further suggestions:

owner of cycle shop

school teacher

County Sports Advisor

grandparent

member of rambling association.

Character Card: Against   Unit 3 (Year 5)

The following characters are against the Vehicle Limitation Act:

Recommended characters:

- daily commuter
- human rights campaigner
- car manufacturer
- parent with young children
- car mechanic.

Further suggestions:

local bus driver

fire officer

second local resident

owner of local garage

shopkeeper.

Individual Character Profiles will offer each pupil a brief summary of his or her character's viewpoint in relation to the scenario, that is, how and why they will be affected by the outcome.

There are a total of ten characters available (five recommended characters from each side), though others may be added if necessary. All pupils in each group must receive a different role – and preferably half the roles will come from Character Card: For and the other half from Character Card Against.

Explain to the pupils what is to happen next. Before the next workshop (Lesson 2), the pupils must spend time developing opinions and constructing arguments in note form, on behalf of their character. Each pupil will need to come to the group prepared to argue for or against the proposed Vehicle Limitation Act – with good reasons to support their arguments.

Lesson 2

Begin with a circle meeting. Revisit the vision statement, core values and group pledges of the preliminary lessons. Reiterate the importance of abiding by the pledges when interacting within the group discussions that follow. Everyone must have a chance to speak AND to listen.

The pupils reform the groups from Lesson 1. Give a copy of the Character Record Sheet to every pupil. Each group member will have a turn to share her opinions and arguments in respect of the proposed bill. Pupils will need to listen carefully to each other's views, noting down the names, roles and a brief two-line summary of the views of the other members in their group. Collect in the record sheets at the end of the session – and check against the original Character Profile cards.

At the end of the session, hold a short plenary in which children are invited to report back to the whole class not on their specific views and arguments, but on the process of sharing opinions – was it helpful to find others with similar views? Was there a sense of different sides forming in the group as people discovered who shared their own views and who did not? Which was easier, expressing one's own viewpoint or listening to the views of another? Did the children find themselves paying more attention to those who shared similar views to their own?

Explain to the pupils the next step in the unit – each pupil is to prepare a letter to their local MP in which they state their own views on the proposed Vehicle Limitation Act. The next workshop will be a 'public meeting' hosted by the local Member for Parliament (that is, the teacher) in which some of the letters be read out formally, after which everyone will have the chance to speak or ask questions.

Lesson 3

The lesson begins with a short group session in which pupils who are playing the same characters across the groups get together to share ideas and thoughts, and prepare a good case. They can refer to their letters for their views if they wish. Each group of 'like-characters' will need to elect a spokesperson (some one different from the spokesperson for Unit 2). The elected speaker will address the class at the following public meeting.

Come together as a class and explain the procedure for the public meeting: there will be a table at the front of the room from which the local MP (the teacher) will chair the meeting. Sitting either side of the Chairperson will be the elected spokespersons (one of every main character from the character cards, that is, five on each side). The format for the meeting can be altered to suit timings and location, but a suggested order might be:

- Chairperson (the teacher) opens the meeting with an explanation of the proposed bill.
- Chairperson invites each of the characters to present their viewpoints, beginning with a supporter of the bill and then alternating between supporters and opposers.

- Chairperson invites comments from the floor – this is an opportunity for other pupils to ask questions or express their views.

- Final vote – for this you will need to distil the different ideas into a shortlist of options. These might include:

    1. Go ahead with the Vehicle Limitation Act

    2. Make amendments to the Vehicle Limitation Act

    3. Replace the bill altogether with an alternative one

    4. Keep the status quo (no need for new bill).

Once the options have been established – all pupils vote for the one they would settle for.

The different characters may well have different views – and it was very important that these were properly heard. However, once the options are listed, pupils will need to consider the question:

> *If I cannot have exactly what I want, what would the next best thing be?*

Lesson 4

This shorter session comprises of a class discussion (out of role), in which all pupils may feedback to the rest of the group their thoughts on the role-play. The meeting can be an informal discussion loosely based around the themes of tolerance, empathy and cooperation, or you may wish to lead the session using the following questions as a guide:

- Was the final decision the right one? How can we tell?

- How would this Act be 'road tested' in real life?

- Which is more important, the needs of individuals or the needs of the environment?

- Which is more important, looking after your children or looking after the world?

- How can we get individuals to see their roles as global citizens?

- Are there any proposed or implemented bills that are currently dividing opinions?

Section 2: Follow-up Activities

Prime Minister's Questions

Video an edition of Prime Minister's questions. Watch and discuss in class. Refer to the following questions: How did the MPs behave? Who was the chairperson (The Speaker) and why was it important to have such a role? Were MPs satisfied with their answers? Did the more controversial questions come from opposition MPs or from members of the PM's own party? Was there some serious debating going on or did it seem like a bit of fun? If you can, record some footage of a new bill being debated in the House and then discuss with the pupils what will happen next (for example, it is debated in House of Lords, amendments made, debated again).

Placards

Inform the children that the Prime Minister is coming to your town. You decide to exercise your right to stage a peaceful protest in opposition to the new Vehicle Limitation Act. Ask the children to consider what sort of slogans they could write on placards and banners. Some examples are: WE NEED OUR CARS! WHERE'S YOUR BIKE? HOW MANY CARS HAVE YOU GOT?

Radio Show

Ask the children to imagine they are on a radio show. In groups of three the pupils prepare a script in which a radio presenter interviews two guests: a local MP in favour of the new bill and a local resident who opposes it. The presenter will need to ask some sensible questions that allow each guest to present her case and then to 'confront' each other.

Leaflet

Ask the children to imagine they are working for Greenpeace. They believe that the new bill is good news for the environment, but they are concerned that if enough people oppose it the government may decide to drop it. Design a promotional flyer (folded A4 sheet) that can be distributed to homes, informing readers of the environmental effects of the rising number of cars and roads in the country – and persuading them to vote for the new bill.

Design Brief

If motor vehicles were scrapped altogether because they were considered to be just too harmful to the environment, what other forms of transport might be available? Ask the pupils to set about designing new ways of travelling, in vehicles that are more sympathetic to the environment. The final design will need to be presented in a non-chronological report (a double-page spread with text and annotated visuals).

Section 3: Curriculum Overview

Curriculum Overview	National Curriculum references
PSHE and Citizenship	1a, 1c, 1e, 2a, 2b, 2f, 2g, 4a, 5a, 5c-e, 5i
English	En1: 1-10, En2: 3b, 3f, 4e, 5a-g, 9a, 9c En3: 1a-e, 2a, 3, 7c, 9c, 9d, 10, 12
NLS Text Types	radio playscripts persuasive: formal letters, placards, leaflets informative: annotated designs.
Mathematics	Ma2: 1a, 1h, 4a, 4b, Ma3: 1a, 1e, 4a
ICT	2a, 2g, 3e, 5a-b, 6e
Art and design	1a-c, 2a, 2c, 4a-b, 5b, 5d
Design and technology	1a, 1b, 1d, 2a-c, 4a, 4c, 5a-b

Context Builder 3	Unit 3 (Year 5)

Context The year is 2015 and the country is in crisis: the problem – cars. The last ten years have seen such a rise in the number of vehicles on our roads, new highways are having to be built, existing roads are being widened and fuel emissions continue to fog the skies. It is time for action.

Scenario The government is proposing to bring in a new bill, The Vehicle Limitation Act, which will limit the number of cars to one per family (excluding works vehicles). Good prices will be paid for surplus cars currently owned, and these will be sold off to other countries with fewer cars. Public transport will be improved and the number of bicycle lanes will be increased. All good news for the environment, but not everyone is happy....

Glossary *Bill* – a draft form of an Act of Parliament, or law.

Fuel emissions – the gases that enter the atmosphere from a car's exhaust.

Character Card: For   Unit 3 (Year 5)

The following characters are in favour of The Vehicle Limitation Act:

Recommended characters:

- wildlife campaigner
- cyclist
- member of Greenpeace
- parent with young children
- family doctor (GP).

Further suggestions:

owner of cycle shop

school teacher

County Sports Advisor

grandparent

member of rambling association.

Character Card: Against   Unit 3 (Year 5)

The following characters are against the Vehicle Limitation Act:

Recommended characters:

- daily commuter
- human rights campaigner
- car manufacturer
- parent with young children
- car mechanic.

Further suggestions:

local bus driver

fire officer

second local resident

owner of local garage

shopkeeper.

Character Profile 1: Wildlife campaigner

The creation of new roads across the country to accommodate for the rise in traffic volume is having a devastating effect on wildlife. Hedgerows, some of which date back centuries, are being ripped up and replaced by tarmac and steel barriers. As a wildlife campaigner you have visited many of the proposed sites for new roads and you have seen with your own eyes the birds and insects that will be displaced. Also, you worry that as the number of cars increases, so the number of animal fatalities will rise as a result of more road accidents. This new bill is essential.

Character Profile 2: Cyclist

Since you decided to sell your car and make the two-mile journey to work by pedal power, you have felt so many benefits. Your health and fitness has risen, you feel less anxious and stressed at work and your wallet is healthier too with no road tax, no insurance, no maintenance bills and no fuel costs. In addition to these benefits you feel positive about your own contribution to preserving the environment – one less car, polluting the atmosphere. If the new bill means less exhaust fumes for you to have to breath in every morning and fewer harassed drivers doing battle with you each day, then it can only be good news.

Character Profile 3: Member of Greenpeace

Fuel emissions entering the atmosphere, green fields being dug up to make way for more roads, congestion, noise pollution, road rage, road accidents and ever diminishing energy sources – this is not really the world you signed up for. And it's time to change it. This new bill may not patch the hole in the ozone layer or prevent the polar ice caps from melting straight away, but it will certainly help to create a more pleasant land for your descendents to live in. It must go ahead.

Character Profile 4: Parent with young children

Making the walk from home to school every morning with your two children is never easy: listening to the drone of passing traffic, breathing in the exhaust fumes and battling to cross the road are not ideal ways for your children to start their day – especially when they see most of your neighbours climbing into their 4 x 4s only to queue up outside the same school gates, cursing because they cannot find a parking space! You worry about child obesity, about the state of the nation's fitness levels, about laziness and apathy, and about the environment in which your children will live, long after you have gone. This bill will go some way towards setting a better example to young people.

Character Profile 5: Family doctor

As a doctor, you have been worried for some time about the general state of the nation's health and fitness. Whether it is through a lack of time or a lack of interest, or both, it seems that more and more people are leading sedentary lives these days – and their health is suffering as a result. Children are being ferried to and from school, a short stroll to the shops is now half-hour search for a parking space and the stress of road rage alone is enough to send patients to an early grave. Dumping the car, getting on a bike or walking to the bus stop must be a good thing.

Character Profile 6: Daily commuter

Working several miles from home, the bike is just not an option. Recently you attempted using public transport instead: the train was late the first day and cancelled the second, and the bus took so long you missed an important meeting! Your wife and children need the car during the working day – so what is the alternative? You would love the luxury of working from home, but it is unlikely your employer would come to you! Driving to work is really the only way you can keep your job.

Character Profile 7: Human rights campaigner

You agree that the environment needs saving and that fuel emissions are not helping, but this proposed law is just taking it too far. The government have been bringing out so many new bills recently, and many of them, like this one, are creating a 'nanny state' – in which the politicians act like nannies, telling us how many toys we are allowed to have in our cots! If we have worked hard to save up enough money to but two cars, then we should be allowed to have them. What will it be next? One TV per family? One bath a week? Three bags of shopping per person?

Character Profile 8: Car manufacturer

This new bill poses a very real threat to your entire company. Halving the number of cars for many families will greatly reduce your sales figures and a vastly reduced demand in the future. This will mean job losses on a massive scale. You could, of course start making bicycles instead, but how many engineers does it take to make a bike, compared to a sports car? Unless the Government are going to compensate you, this bill must not go through.

Character Profile 9: Parent of young child

Your partner leaves every morning for work. It is essential that he or she has the car because they work some distance away. Your child has now reached school age and so you recently purchased a small car to do the school run every morning. You live several miles from school and to walk and use the bus would mean your child having such a long day – and the cost would be twice as much too. If this law is made, you will have to face a very real dilemma – who will get to use the remaining car?

Character Profile 10: Car mechanic

Patching up ozone layers and reducing fuel emissions to save the planet is all very well but as a car mechanic what are you expected to fix when all the cars have disappeared – bikes? A lot of people depend on the car industry for their livelihood; whether you make cars or make a living from fixing them, this bill can only spell the beginning of the end.
You feel sure there are other ways of saving the planet than by pushing yet more people out of jobs and into the growing 'dole' queues.

Character Record Sheet

Name..................................

Pupil name:
Character role:
Views:

Pupil name:
Character role:
Views:

Pupil name:
Character role:
Views:

Pupil name:
Character role:
Views:

Pupil name:
Character role:
Views:

Bad Weather

Section 1: Lesson Plans

Lesson 1

Arrange a circle meeting for the whole class. Introduce the theme for the unit by reading out the following Context Builder 4 (also enclosed at the end of this unit for photocopying).

Context Builder 4	Unit 4 (Year 6)

Context	A freak blizzard during the night has left treacherous conditions on the roads surrounding a small town. Snow drifts, icy patches and even some fallen trees have left some residents stranded at home, while others are battling to get to work and to school.
Scenario	It is 7.15am and at the town's largest primary school, the small team of staff who have managed to appear face a difficult decision – remain open or close? The car park is an ice rink, various water pipes have frozen and there are signs of more snow to come. Closing would mean many parents would not be able to go to work, having to stay with their children at home, and what about those who have already set off? Yet staying open would mean all those hazardous journeys that could have been avoided if the children had stayed in bed; and what if the children end up stranded at school, with their parents unable to reach them?
Glossary	*Blizzard* – a severe snowstorm with high winds *Hazardous* – risky or dangerous.

Elicit pupils' initial thoughts about how bad weather can affect the daily routines of ordinary people. Consider the dangers involved in making journeys in hazardous conditions. Focus on how weather can affect the infrastructure of a local community – roads, services, heating, lighting or food supplies.

Then encourage the children to consider the implications of remaining open or closing the school. How would people be directly affected by this decision? How might people react if the school were to be closed? If it is assumed that the school secretary could contact everyone to inform them of the closure, would everyone be happy?

Initiate a discussion about the importance of respecting other people's views and responding to others' ideas sensitively and appropriately. Emphasize the importance of identifying common aims – that is, to provide the best possible care for the children at all times.

When everyone has had the chance to contribute, establish the groups for the unit. You may wish to record the names in each group for future lessons. Then read out the following Character Cards (also at the end of this unit), and give each pupil a role to play.

Character Card: For   Unit 4 (Year 6)

The following characters are in favour of closing the school:

Recommended characters:

- school caretaker
- after school club coordinator
- road-crossing supervisor
- parent-teacher with two pupils at the school
- catering supervisor.

Further suggestions:

health and safety officer

parent (and road traffic police officer)

local resident

school governor

retired teacher.

Character Card: Against   Unit 4 (Year 6)

The following characters are against closing the school:

Recommended characters:

- teacher (with son at another school)
- school secretary
- head of music staff
- mother of reception pupil
- father of Year 5 pupil.

Further suggestions:

school governor

local resident

Year 4 teacher

parent (and childminder)

football coach.

Individual Character Profiles will offer each pupil a brief summary of his or her character's viewpoint in relation to the scenario – that is, how and why they will be affected by the outcome.

There are a total of ten characters available (five recommended characters from each side), though others may be added if necessary. All pupils in each group must receive a different role – and preferably half the roles will come from Character Card: For and the other half from Character Card Against.

Explain to the pupils what is to happen next: before the next workshop (Lesson 2), the pupils must spend time developing opinions and constructing arguments in bullet points, on behalf of their character. Each pupil will need to come to the group prepared to argue for or against closing the school for the day – with good reasons to support their arguments.

Lesson 2

Begin with a circle meeting. Revisit the vision statement, core values and group pledges of the preliminary lessons. Reiterate the importance of abiding by the pledges when interacting within the group discussions that follow. Everyone must have a chance to speak and to listen.

The pupils reform the groups from Lesson 1. Give a copy of the Character Record Sheet to every pupil. Each group member will have a turn to share their views on the plan to close the school for the day. Pupils will need to listen carefully to each others' ideas, noting down the names, roles and a brief two-line summary of the views of the other members in their group. Collect in the record sheets at the end of the session and check them against the original Character Profile cards.

At the end of the session, hold a short plenary in which children are invited to report back to the whole class not on their specific views and arguments, but on the process of sharing opinions – was it helpful to find others with similar views? Was there a sense of different sides forming in the group as people discovered who shared their own views and who did not? Which was easier, expressing one's own viewpoint or listening to the views of another? Did the children find themselves paying more attention to those who shared similar views to their own?

Explain to the pupils the next step in the unit – each pupil is to prepare a brief announcement that could be read out on local radio, informing parents of the plan to close or keep the school open, and giving reasons why this decision has been reached. The next workshop will be a general 'emergency' meeting chaired by the fictional school's head teacher (that is, the teacher) in which the bullet points from Lesson 1 and the radio announcements from this lesson can be referred to when characters come to defend their views.

Lesson 3

The lesson begins with a short group session in which pupils who are playing the same characters across the groups get together to share ideas and thoughts, and prepare a good argument. They can refer to their bullet points or radio announcements for their views if they wish. Each group of 'like-characters' will need to elect a spokesperson (someone different from the spokesperson for Unit 3). The elected speaker will address the class at the following public meeting.

Come together as a class and explain the procedure for the emergency meeting: there will be a table at the front of the room from which the local head teacher (the teacher) will chair the meeting. Sitting either side of the Chairperson will be the elected spokespersons (one of every recommended character from the character cards, that is, five on each side). The format for the meeting can be altered to suit timings and location, but a suggested order might be:

- Chairperson (the teacher) opens the meeting with an explanation of the difficulties the weather is causing and the possible plan to close the school;

- Chairperson invites each of the characters to present their viewpoints, beginning with someone in favour of closing the school for the day and then alternating between those who agree and those who disagree;

- Chairperson invites comments from the floor – this is an opportunity for other pupils to ask questions or express their views;

- Final vote – for this you will need to distil the different ideas into a shortlist of options. These might include:

  1. Go ahead and close the school for the day

  2. Remain open.

  3. Close but try to arrange lift sharing and child minding for parents who need it.

  4. Inform parents that the school will remain open but attendance is 'at the discretion of parents' – children attend if they can.

  5. Send pupils to a neighbouring school for the day.

Once the options have been established – all pupils vote for the one they would settle for.

The different characters may well have different views – and it was very important that these were properly heard. However, once the options are listed, pupils will need to consider the question:

If I cannot have exactly what I want, what would the next best thing be?

Lesson 4

This shorter session comprises of a class discussion (out of role), in which all pupils may feedback to the rest of the group their thoughts on the role-play. The meeting can be an informal discussion loosely based around the themes of tolerance, empathy and cooperation, or you may wish to lead the session using the following questions as a guide:

- Which decision was the safest one?

- How can we ever really plan for unpredictable weather?

- How important was it that the school made a decision quickly?

- Does your own school have an emergency procedure for such scenarios?

- How important is it that people cooperate in these situations?

- Can you think of other situations where a school might have to close in this way? What would you do?

Section 2: Follow-Up Activities

Geography Study

Conduct a research project into the weather in your local area – have there been any instances when schools have had to close? Use the internet or library archives to compile a fact file that shows weather records for the area, including: the most rain ever recorded, the deepest snow, the strongest winds. Which area of the country receives the most snow or rain? Which areas have a temperate climate? Consider how people adjust their way of life to adapt to the extreme climates in which they live.

Poetry

Write your own poem(s) about extreme weather. You may wish to write about a snow storm or a blizzard, or perhaps the day when rain stopped play – a football match was cancelled perhaps. Try to describe how the weather impacts on your own life; how does it make you feel?

Story

Write a story in which an extreme weather change like the one featured above forces your school to close. What do you do instead – how might you spend your day? You could call your story, 'A Snowy Adventure'.

You may wish to plan your story by designing a storyboard in which you present the scenes from the story in pictorial form with captions underneath.

Newspaper

Imagine you are a reporter with a local newspaper. A number of schools in the area have had to close because of poor weather conditions. Local roads have been blocked and some residents are without electricity. The weekly local newspaper is due out at the end of the week and you have been given the task of writing a feature for the front page on the extraordinary weather changes that the town has just endured. You will need to think of a good headline, perhaps: 'The Day the Heavens Opened'.

Section 3: Curriculum Overview

Curriculum Overview	National Curriculum references
PSHE and Citizenship	1a, 1c, 2a, 2e, 2f, 2h, 2j, 4a, 5a, 5c-e, 5g
English	En1: 1-7, En2: 3b-g, 5a-g, 9a, 9c En3: 1a-e, 2a, 3, 7c, 9c, 9d, 10, 12
NLS Text Types	story poems journalistic recount informative text (Geography study).
Mathematics	Ma4: 1a, 1f, 2b-d
Geography	1b-c, 2d, 3a, 3d, 7a-b
ICT	1a, 1b, 3b, 5a, 5b

Context Builder 4	Unit 4 (Year 6)

Context   A freak blizzard during the night has left treacherous conditions on the roads surrounding a small town. Snow drifts, icy patches and even some fallen trees have left some residents stranded at home, while others are battling to get to work and to school.

Scenario   It is 7.15am and at the town's largest primary school, the small team of staff who have managed to appear face a difficult decision – remain open or close? The car park is an ice rink, various water pipes have frozen and there are signs of more snow to come. Closing would mean many parents would not be able to go to work, having to stay with their children at home, and what about those who have already set off? Yet staying open would mean all those hazardous journeys that could have been avoided if the children had stayed in bed; and what if the children end up stranded at school, with their parents unable to reach them?

Glossary   *Blizzard* – a severe snowstorm with high winds

Hazardous – risky or dangerous.

Character Card: For — Unit 4 (Year 6)

The following characters are in favour of closing the school:

Recommended characters:

- school caretaker
- after school club coordinator
- road-crossing supervisor
- parent-teacher with two pupils at the school
- catering supervisor.

Further suggestions:

health and safety officer

parent (and road traffic police officer)

local resident

school governor

retired teacher.

Character Card: Against — Unit 4 (Year 6)

The following characters are against closing the school:

Recommended characters:

- teacher (with son at another school)
- school secretary
- head of music staff
- mother of reception pupil
- father of Year 5 pupil.

Further suggestions:

school governor

local resident

Year 4 teacher

former school inspector

parent (and personal injury lawyer).

Character Profile 1: School Caretaker

Since early this morning, you have been out there with your barrow load of grit and shovel, trying desperately to make the footpaths and car parks safe under foot; but the job is simply too great. If anyone slips and breaks a limb, it will be your fault for not gritting that particular part of pavement properly. The responsibility is immense! Added to this fact is that there are frozen pipes around the school that are causing problems with the water system. It is going to be difficult enough trying to sort out this mess without having hundreds of children running around, injuring themselves with snowballs!

Character Profile 2: After school club coordinator

As the person responsible for looking after the children at the end of the day, you often find yourself delayed in getting home because you are stuck with two or three pupils, whose parents are equally delayed in picking them up. If the school stays open in this weather, it won't be two or three late arrivals, it will be dozens. You might as well bring your sleeping bag in fact. Surely it is safer to quit while you're ahead and close now.

Character Profile 3: Road crossing supervisor

Navigating the busy stretch of road outside the school gates is hard enough on a normal day, with the traffic that hurtles past and the children that will insist on running into the road without looking, but with the patches of black ice today, surely it will be a death trap. The responsibility of getting the children safely across the road with all the sliding cars about is simply too great. It is too risky for the children to be anywhere other than safely tucked up in their living rooms (which is where you'd like to be right now).

Character Profile 4: Health and safety officer

You know that there are some parents already on their way – and their children will have to be catered for. You know also that there will be a great many parents who may be inconvenienced by having their children at home on a working day. However, your prime concern is for the safety of the children while they are on the school premises and for this reason alone, you must send them home. Parents will be irritated by the closure, but they would be a great deal more concerned if their children slipped and injured themselves whilst at school. The weather has rendered the buildings and grounds in such a condition that you cannot provide the first class care that you usually do.

Character Profile 5: Catering supervisor

With several frozen pipes and the prospect of children stranded at school for some time, the day, like the weather, is looking bleak. If the snow gets worse, you may have to have children in school for many hours, while their parents find ways of reaching them. This means that it will fall to you to supply them with the all-important nourishment in this cold weather – and that might mean much more than lunch. With several staff already called in to say they cannot get to school, you are down to a skeleton staff in the kitchens. Also the delivery of vegetables that was due early this morning, looks like it might not make it. Closing is the only option – or its crackers and cheese all round.

Character Profile 6: Parent (with son at another school)

You have recently received confirmation from your elder son's school that they will be opening as usual today. You can see no reason why your younger son's primary school cannot do the same. Your son will be frustrated and bored at home on his own and that will lead to mischief! Provided he is sensible when walking around outside, he should have fun in the snow. Keeping children indoors when the weather is too cold is not going to help them grow into strong, resilient young adults. You have to make the special trip out for your elder son, and the primary school is only down the road.

Character Profile 7: School secretary

The number of telephone calls that will need to be made to close the school for the day is almost infinite – and there is little time left anyway. Last time you had to close the school there were so many parents who were inconvenienced and many were quick to express their feelings to you over the phone. You felt like it was your fault, and the prospect of making the same calls again does not fill with you with enthusiasm.

Character Profile 8: Head of music staff

You have a large number of peripatetic music staff operating in the school, some of whom travel some distance to get here, and all of whom depend very much on teaching their private lessons for their income. Cancelling a whole day's lessons and telling them they are not required today will mean staff losing out financially. Most of them teach in other schools on other days, so rescheduling cancelled lessons is not really an option.

Character Profile 9: Mother of reception pupil

As a working parent you have many commitments during the week and today is no exception. If there is the slightest chance that the school could function despite the weather, then they should certainly remain open. You feel sure that your child will be perfectly safe – the care she has received so far at the school has been first class after all. If they send the children home, it will be very difficult for many parents to find someone to look after them. Unfortunately the meetings you have scheduled for today simply cannot be moved. People are depending on you (at home and at work!)

Character Profile 10: Father of Year 4 pupil

Playing around in the snow is part of growing up. You can remember many days when your own school years ago was struck by bad weather – such times were the best you had at school! Pulling together, helping each other and making the best of a situation is all part of children's education – or it should be. You hope very much that the health and safety officers in the area do not feel that they must close schools down for the day for fear of someone slipping over and claiming compensation. Your daughter is packed and raring to get there!

Character Record Sheet

Name...................................

Pupil name:
Character role:
Views:

Pupil name:
Character role:
Views:

Pupil name:
Character role:
Views:

Pupil name:
Character role:
Views:

Pupil name:
Character role:
Views:

Last Train To Paxton

Section 1: Lesson Plans

Lesson 1

Organise a circle meeting for the class. Introduce the theme for the unit by reading out the following Context Builder 5 (a photocopiable version is enclosed at the end of this unit).

Context Builder 5	**Unit 5 (Year 6)**

Context	The village of Paxton has boasted its own railway station for more than one hundred years. In its heyday, each steam train pulled many carriages, each one bursting with commuters, day trippers and railway enthusiasts – but sadly those days are gone. Records show that barely any tickets are now sold at Paxton – in fact its line is known locally as the ghost train. But, to the handful of faithful passengers it is a lifeline.
Scenario	Cross-Country Trains (CCT), the company who maintain the line at Paxton have announced plans to close the station and redevelop the land because it is no longer cost effective. Together in partnership with the local council, they plan to build much needed public car park and a restaurant on the site, to cater for the growing number of tourists that visit the village by car each year.
Glossary	*Heyday* – a period of great success – when things were going well. *Cost effective* – making enough money to keep going.

Elicit pupils' initial thoughts about the role of the railway in the village. Think about how important the station is to the local community. If ticket sales are falling so much, is it worth maintaining? Discuss the term 'heyday' – ask the pupils to imagine a time when railways were used much more than they are now, when the Paxton Station would have been a thriving place, full of workers, day trippers and so on. Consider ways in which the station and platform might still be important to some people, despite its falling number of visitors.

Consider the term 'cost effective': what exactly does this mean in relation to the station? Think about the cost of employing its staff, maintaining the buildings and so on offset against the revenue from selling tickets. Is making a profit the station's only purpose? Are there other aspects that might be worth subsidising, like local history, heritage, education?

Consider the idea of parking in this village – focus on the difficulties that popular villages like this may have in the summer months, when they are swamped with cars. Would a new car park be useful? Perhaps it would attract even more tourists into the village, and this might be good news for local businesses.

When everyone has had the chance to contribute, establish the groups for the unit. You may wish to record the names in each group for future lessons. Then read out the following Character Cards (also enclosed at the end of the unit for photocopying), and give each pupil a role to play.

Character Card: For   Unit 5 (Year 6)

The following characters are in favour of closing the station at Paxton:

Recommended characters:

- local resident (with house next to line)
- local car user
- shop keeper in village
- tourist
- member of local council.

Further suggestions:

local parent with young children

car mechanic

local wildlife enthusiast

young married person (looking for restaurants)

local shopper.

Character Card: Against   Unit 5 (Year 6)

The following characters are against closing the station at Paxton:

Recommended characters:

- rail commuter
- local historian and rail enthusiast
- local resident
- restaurant owner in village
- station master.

Further suggestions:

parent with young children

local resident and former railway worker

local railway engineer

member of local Ramblers' Association

local park keeper.

Individual Character Profiles (included at the end of the unit) will offer each pupil a brief summary of his or her character's viewpoint in relation to the scenario, that is, how and why they will be affected by the outcome.

There are a total of ten characters available (five recommended characters from each side), though others may be added if necessary. All pupils in each group must receive a different role – and preferably half the roles will come from Character Card: For and the other half from Character Card Against, though others may be added if necessary.

Explain to the pupils what is to happen next: before the next workshop (Lesson 2), the pupils must spend time developing opinions and constructing arguments in bullet points, on behalf of their character. Each pupil will need to come to the group ready to support the closure of the station or argue against it, with good reasons in support. They will need to consider how the decision will impact on their character, but also on how they can put forward arguments that refer to the needs of others too. The most successful arguments will be those that consider the greatest number of people (rather than just an individual character's own needs).

Lesson 2

Begin with a circle meeting. Revisit the vision statement, core values and group pledges of the preliminary lessons. Reiterate the importance of abiding by the pledges when interacting within the group discussions that follow. Everyone must have a chance to speak and to listen.

The pupils reform the groups from Lesson 1. Give a copy of the Character Record Sheet (at the end of this unit) to every pupil. Each group member will have a turn to share their views on the plan to close down the station at Paxton and build a public car park and restaurant. Pupils will need to listen carefully to each others' ideas, noting down the names, roles and a brief two-line summary of the views of the other members in their group. Collect in the record sheets at the end of the session – and check against the original Character Profile cards.

At the end of the session, hold a short plenary in which children are invited to report back to the whole class not on their specific views and arguments, but on the process of sharing opinions – was it helpful to find others with similar views? Was there a sense of different sides forming in the group as people discovered who shared their own views and who did not? Which was easier, expressing one's own viewpoint or listening to the views of another? Did the children find themselves paying more attention to those who shared similar views to their own?

Explain to the pupils the next step in the unit – each pupil is to prepare a formal letter to the local council, either supporting the plan to close the station at Paxton, or opposing it, stating why the station should remain as a going concern. The next workshop will be a general meeting hosted by the Chairperson of the local council (that is, the teacher) in which the bullet points from Lesson 1 and the formal letters from this lesson can be referred to when characters come to defend their views.

Lesson 3

The lesson begins with a short group session in which pupils who are playing the same characters across the groups get together to share ideas and thoughts, and prepare a good argument in favour or opposing the new plans for Paxton Station. They can refer to their bullet points or letters for their views if they wish. Each group of 'like-characters' will need to elect a spokesperson (some one different from the spokesperson for Unit 4). The elected speaker will address the class at the following public meeting.

Come together as a class and explain the procedure for the public meeting: there will be a table at the front of the room from which the Chairperson (the teacher) will host the meeting. Sitting either side of the Chairperson will be the elected spokespersons (one of every main character from the character cards: five on each side). The format for the meeting can be altered to suit timings and location, but a suggested order might be:

- Chairperson (the teacher) opens the meeting by explaining the plans to close the Paxton Station, redirect the railway line, build a public car park on the site and rebuild the station house as a new restaurant

- Chairperson invites each of the characters to present their viewpoints, beginning with someone in favour of closing the station and then alternating between those who agree and those who disagree

- Chairperson invites comments from the floor – this is an opportunity for other pupils to ask questions or express their views

- Final vote – for this you will need to distil the different ideas into a shortlist of options. These might include:

  1. Close the Paxton Station and build the car park and restaurant on its site.

  2. Keep the station open and running, subsidised by the council.

  3. Keep the station open and running but find an alternative site for the new car park. Set up a charity to maintain the railway.

  4. As above, but the local villagers form a consortium to take over the costs of running the station.

  5. As above, but establish a 'museum of locomotion' next to the railway to bring in some extra income.

Once the options have been established – all pupils vote for the one they would settle for.

The different characters may well have different views – and it was very important that these were properly heard. However, once the options are listed, pupils will need to consider the question:

If I cannot have exactly what I want, what would the next best thing be?

Lesson 4

This shorter session comprises a class discussion (out of role), in which all pupils may feedback to the rest of the group their thoughts on the role-play. The meeting can be an informal discussion loosely based around the themes of tolerance, empathy and cooperation, or you may wish to lead the session using the following questions as a guide:

- How could we tell which viewpoint was the 'right' one?

- Which is more important, preserving our heritage or making a profit?

- Were we able to separate our own individual interests from the needs of the village as a whole?

- Are there any other options that might keep more people happy?

- If the station was closed, how could disgruntled people make their views known then?

Section 2: Follow-Up Activities

History Study

Conduct a history project in which you look at the role of the railways in your local area over the last hundred years. Try to assess if and why the railways have become less used nowadays. Write a chronological report on a local railway through the ages.

Art Project

Paint or draw two artistic impressions of Paxton Station: one set on 1895 and the other in the present day. What features would be different? If the buildings are exactly the same, how else might you show the period?

Poem

Write a poem entitled 'The Disused Railway' in which you describe an imaginary railway station, long neglected and forgotten. Try to paint a vivid picture of not only the appearance of the buildings and signs, but also of the atmosphere and mood of the place. Refer to the memories of happier times that sweep through the hollow platform.

Newspaper Report

Imagine you are a reporter with a local newspaper, responsible for covering the news story of the closure of Paxton Station. Report on the proposed plan, including a picture of the station now and another of the site once the new plans have gone ahead. Try to include interviews with local parties, some in favour, others against the plans. What might your headline be? Some examples are: 'Last Train To Paxton', 'End of An Era' and 'A Sign of the Times'.

Section 3: Curriculum Overview

Curriculum Overview	National Curriculum references
PSHE and Citizenship	1a, 1e, 2a, 2d, 2f, 2h, 2k, 4a, 4b, 5a, 5c-e,
English	En1: 1-4, 8c, 11a; En2: 3a, 3e-g, 5f, 9c En3: 1a-e, 2a-c, 3, 7c, 9c, 9d, 10, 12
NLS Text Types	poems story chronological report journalistic recount.
Geography	1a-e, 2a, 2d, 3a, 3d, 5a, 5b, 7a-b
History	5a-b, 7, 11a
ICT	1a, 1b, 2c, 3b, 5a, 5b

Context Builder 5	Unit 5 (Year 6)

Context   The village of Paxton has boasted its own railway station for more than one hundred years. In its heyday, each steam train pulled many carriages, each one bursting with commuters, day trippers and railway enthusiasts – but sadly those days are gone. Records show that barely any tickets are now sold at Paxton – in fact its line is known locally as the ghost train. But, to the handful of faithful passengers it is a lifeline.

Scenario   Cross-Country Trains (CCT), the company who maintain the line at Paxton have announced plans to close the station and redevelop the land because it is no longer cost effective. Together in partnership with the local council, they plan to build much needed public car park and a restaurant on the site, to cater for the growing number of tourists that visit the village by car each year.

Glossary   *Heyday* – a period of great success – when things were going well

Cost effective – making enough money to keep going.

Character Card: For   Unit 5 (Year 6)

The following characters are in favour of closing the station at Paxton:

Recommended characters:

- local resident (with house next to line)
- local car user
- shop keeper in village
- tourist
- member of local council.

Further suggestions:

local parent with young children

car mechanic

local wildlife enthusiast

young married person (looking for restaurants)

local shopper.

Character Card: Against   Unit 5 (Year 6)

The following characters are against closing the station at Paxton:

Recommended characters:

- rail commuter
- local historian and rail enthusiast
- local resident
- restaurant owner in village
- station master.

Further suggestions:

parent with young children

local resident and former railway worker

local railway engineer

member of local Ramblers' Association

local park keeper.

Character Profile 1: Local resident

Many locals have expressed sadness at the thought of losing their station at Paxton. They like the quaint station house, the picket fences, the little Paxton signs that line the station walls. Some even use the train occasionally, but few of them actually live next to the line, like you do. The trains zip past the back of your garden, and since the old steam engines were replaced with high-speed diesels, the sound is anything but quaint! One day you will want to sell your house, and with an active railway track just metres away from your kitchen windows, it won't be easy. Closing Paxton station and redirecting the line can only mean good news for residents like yourself.

Character Profile 2: Local car user

Paxton village is a pleasant place, with all the shops you would need, but if there's one thing it badly lacks it's a car park. In the summer time especially, when the tourists come to take their photographs of the quintessential village green, the whole place is gridlocked with cars and there is no room left for the locals. Despite living here for some years you have only used the Paxton train once or twice and so closing the station and replacing it with a car park and restaurant would be great news.

Character Profile 3: Shopkeeper in village

Each day you gaze out of your shop window as numerous motorists try to find somewhere to park so that they can visit your store. Many are unable to do so and they have little choice but to drive on, probably to the next village. If you had a car park in the centre of the village, on the site of the railway station, you feel sure that you would see more people coming through your door, bringing some much needed business. More car parking spaces means potentially more visitors, and more customers for all the shops in the village centre. Closing the flagging railway is good news for you.

Character Profile 4: Tourist

You recently visited the village of Paxton, famed for its pretty village green and tea shops. Through the car window you saw a very picturesque place, but sadly that was the only glimpse you had of Paxton, as there was simply nowhere to stop. Instead, the tide of traffic swept you along and before you knew it you were through and out of the other side! You would like to go back again, but unless they do something about parking in the area, you won't bother.

Character Profile 5: Member of local council

You feel sure that the village, with its pretty antique shops, village green and duck pond would attract lots of business in the summer months, but local shop owners all complain that there is nowhere for their customers to park. The station isn't used any more. In its heyday it may well have brought in visitors from far afield, but today most people travel under their own steam and so it really is a waste of valuable land in the village centre. Redirecting the railway, building a car park and turning the station house into a restaurant would solve so many problems for the village community.

Character Profile 6: Rail commuter

Though there may not be many fellow passengers on the platform every morning, to you, the little station at Paxton is a lifeline, and the only way you can get to work. Closing it down would mean you would have to travel to the next station along the line and this is seven miles away. You do not have your own car and the bus service is not frequent enough for you to catch the train you need in the early mornings. Paxton station simply must remain in service.

Character Profile 7: Local historian and rail enthusiast

There are few original railway stations left in the area, and Paxton is one of the oldest. Rail enthusiasts across the county regard the station house and platform in the village as the jewel in the crown, locally. The Victorian station house, with its original fixtures and fittings, the guards' room, the original railway signs all create a nostalgia that must be preserved. Rather than close it all down, you and your fellow enthusiasts think it should be carefully maintained, and perhaps a small museum added to chronicle the important role that the railways played in the local area for generations of villagers. Replacing all this history with a car park, well... it just doesn't bear thinking about.

Character Profile 8: Local resident

As a local resident in the village you are becoming increasingly concerned about the number of visitors that arrive in the centre daily during the tourist season, clogging up the roads, leaving litter around and disturbing the tranquillity of the place. And now, you hear there is a plan to do away with one of the village's oldest and most treasured places in order to make way for a car park that will cater for yet more tourists? It seems such a shame! The original station may not see much action these days, but its pretty buildings and original signs are a lot better than a blanket of tarmac, dotted with pay and display machines.

Character Profile 9: Restaurant owner in village

As the owner of the restaurant that overlooks the village green, you enjoy a comfortable living throughout the year. Despite more pubs opening up around the local area, you still manage to pull in the customers. However, news of a new restaurant to be built in the station house means a potential loss of trade for you. Is there enough business to go around? Besides, throughout the summer you operate a package deal with the local railway that offers travellers a day out on the train, stopping at your restaurant for lunch. Closing the station will put an end to this valuable source of income. Which one of your valued staff will you have to make redundant first?

Character Profile 10: Station Master

You have been assured that, although the station at Paxton may be closed, there will still be a job for you elsewhere on the line – but where? The nearest station is seven miles away and they already have a station-master. How far will you have to travel to work and what will you be doing when you get there? Will you be mending railway tracks twenty miles away? You became the station-master at Paxton fourteen years ago, upon the retirement of your father. The new plan would mean the end of an era for your family.

Character Record Sheet

Name.......................................

Pupil name:	
Character role:	
Views:	

Pupil name:	
Character role:	
Views:	

Pupil name:	
Character role:	
Views:	

Pupil name:	
Character role:	
Views:	

Pupil name:	
Character role:	
Views:	

Olympic Bid

Section 1: Lesson Plans

Lesson 1

Set up a circle meeting in class. Introduce the theme for the unit by reading out the following Context Builder 6 (enclosed also at the end of this unit).

Context Builder 6	Unit 6 (Year 6)
Context	Your city has beaten its rivals to become the nation's main bid to host a future Olympic Games. If the city is chosen by the International Olympic Committee (IOC) then a major building programme would be necessary, costing the city, and the nation, many millions of pounds – but the fame and notoriety gained from staging this world class event may be worth it. Opinion is divided.
Scenario	Preparing for the Games would bring new jobs, new sports facilities, new transport systems and so on. The gain in tourism too, as the world's media turns its spotlight towards the city, would be significant. Nevertheless, not everyone is backing the bid with some believing that the cost of staging this major event would mean other more urgent and deserving causes within the city, such as hospitals, education and housing would be neglected.
Glossary	*Olympic Games* – a sports competition in which many countries of the world come together to compete in many different events.
	Bid – a submission to the Olympic International Committee to stage the Olympic Games in the city.

Elicit pupils' existing knowledge and experience of the Olympics. How big an event is it? How important might such a bid be to the prosperity of a city – or of a country?

Think about the advantages of hosting such a world event – consider the benefits to the people of the city, and of the country (for example, raising awareness of the place as a holiday destination and improving the infrastructure of a city or building excellent sporting facilities that will last well beyond the Games).

Consider just what might be involved in preparing for an event on this scale – the amount of work that would need to be carried out and, most importantly, the huge expense that would need to be met. Should the money be spent on other things perhaps? What should a city's priorities be? Is sport really that important?

Then consider what people in the local area, and across the country, might think about the Olympic bid. It sounds very exciting but would everyone be in favour? What reasons might people have for objecting? Try to consider how a major event of this kind might impact on the lives of the individuals who live in the host city or country. When everyone has had the chance to contribute, establish the groups for the unit. You may wish to record the names in each group for future lessons. Then read out the following Character Cards (also enclosed at the end of the unit for photocopying), and give each pupil a role to play.

Character Card: For	**Unit 6 (Year 6)**

The following characters support the city's Olympic bid:

Recommended characters:

- member of tourist board
- parent with young children
- hotel owner
- sports coach
- headteacher of local comprehensive school.

Further suggestions:

transport worker

local MP (Member of Parliament)

unemployed resident

manager of local swimming club

representative from the chamber of commerce.

Character Card: Against	**Unit 6 (Year 6)**

The following characters oppose the Olympic bid:

Recommended characters:

- housing officer
- local resident
- hospital manager
- local commuter
- theatre director.

Further suggestions:

road safety officer

resident of rival city

wildlife campaigner

local resident

schools inspector.

Individual Character Profiles (included at the end of the unit) will offer each pupil a brief summary of his or her character's viewpoint in relation to the scenario – that is, how and why they will be affected by the outcome.

There are a total of ten characters available (five recommended characters from each side) though others may be added if necessary. All pupils in each group must receive a different role – and preferably half the roles will come from Character Card: For and the other half from Character Card Against.

Explain to the pupils what is to happen next: before the next workshop (Lesson 2), the pupils must spend time developing opinions and constructing arguments in bullet points, on behalf of their character. Each pupil will need to come to the group ready to support or oppose the plan to host the Olympic Games in the city, with good reasons in support. They will need to consider how the decision will impact on their character, but also on how they can put forward arguments that refer to the needs of others too. The most successful arguments will be those that consider the greatest number of people (rather than just an individual's own needs).

Lesson 2

Begin with a circle meeting. Revisit the vision statement, core values and group pledges of the preliminary lessons. Reiterate the importance of abiding by the pledges when interacting within the group discussions that follow. Everyone must have a chance to speak and to listen.

The pupils reform the groups from Lesson 1. Give a copy of the Character Record Sheet (at the end of the unit) to every pupil. Each group member will have a turn to share their views on the plan to host the Games in the city. Pupils will need to listen carefully to each others' ideas, noting down the names, roles and a brief two-line summary of the views of the other members in their group. Collect in the record sheets at the end of the session – and check against the original Character Profile cards.

At the end of the session, hold a short plenary in which children are invited to report back to the whole class not on their specific views and arguments, but on the process of sharing opinions – was it helpful to find others with similar views? Was there a sense of different sides forming in the group as people discovered who shared their own views and who did not? Which was easier, expressing one's own viewpoint or listening to the views of another? Did the children find themselves paying more attention to those who shared similar views to their own?

Explain to the pupils the next step in the unit: the local newspaper is running a feature on 'What the people think' in relation to the proposed Olympics bid. They will be featuring readers' letters in favour and against the plan. The pupils must write a letter that is good enough to appear in the newspaper, in which they express their viewpoint formally and persuasively.

The next workshop will be a general meeting hosted by a representative from the nation's own Olympic Committee (the teacher) in which the views of the people will be heard prior to taking the bid to the IOC (International Olympic Committee) itself. In this session, pupils will be able to refer to both the bullet points from Lesson 1 and the formal letters from this session.

Lesson 3

The lesson begins with a short group session in which pupils who are playing the same characters across the groups get together to share ideas and thoughts, and prepare a good argument in favour or opposing the new Olympics bid. They can refer to their bullet points or letters for their views if they wish. Each group of 'like-characters' will need to elect a spokesperson (some one different from the spokesperson for Unit 5). The elected speaker will address the class at the following public meeting.

Come together as a class and explain the procedure for the public meeting, there will be a table at the front of the room from which the Olympic representative (the teacher) will chair the meeting. Sitting either side of the Chairperson will be the elected spokespersons (one of every recommended character from character cards, that is, five on each side). The format for the meeting can be altered to suit timings and location, but a suggested order might be:

- Chairperson (the teacher) opens the meeting by introducing the bid to host the Olympic Games in the city in the near future (you may wish to insert a year here).

- Chairperson invites each of the characters to present their viewpoints, beginning with someone in favour of the bid and then alternating between those who agree and those who disagree.

- Chairperson invites comments from the floor – this is an opportunity for other pupils to ask questions or express their views.

- Final vote – for this you will need to distil the different ideas into a shortlist of options. These might include:

  1. Keep backing the bid to host the Olympics in the city.

  2. Support a new bid to share the Olympics with a neighbouring city, thereby spreading the cost.

  3. Drop the plans to host the Olympics in this city and support a different bid from another city.

  4. Drop the plans to host the Olympics in this city, support another city's bid and push to hold a different international event in the city in the future, for example, Commonwealth Games, International Music Festival or Dance Festival etc.

Once the options have been established – all pupils vote for the one they would settle for.

The different characters may well have different views – and it was very important that these were properly heard. However, once the options have been listed, pupils will need to consider the question:

If I cannot have exactly what I want, what would the next best thing be?

Lesson 4

This shorter session comprises of a class discussion (out of role), in which all pupils may feedback to the rest of the group their thoughts on the role-play. The meeting can be an informal discussion loosely based around the themes of tolerance, empathy and cooperation, or you may wish to lead the session using the following questions as a guide:

- How difficult was it to see every side of the story?

- Was it difficult trying to see past the initial excitement that surrounds the Games?

- Were there some views that might have seemed more important than others? Were they?

- Would a city have priorities for their spending plans? What might they be – health, family, housing? Or sport? Which do you think is more important?

Section 2: Follow-Up Activities

Olympics

Research, using the internet and library resources, the last time your at home country hosted the Olympic Games. How successful were they? What changes were made to the main host city to prepare for the Games? Think about changes in the physical and human environment. Are there any Olympic facilities that are still used today? What sort of long-term benefits has the city seen from hosting the Games? Was it all worthwhile? If possible, try to gain primary source material from people who experienced the Games first hand. Write up your findings in a recount.

History of Games

Find out more about the history of the Olympic Games: when was it first the held, and where? How have the Games changed over the years? Have the Games become bigger, with more competitors? Which events are historic and which are relatively new. You may wish to present your findings in a project folder entitled A Torch Through The Ages. Include a timeline in your project.

Geography

Find out where the Olympic Games have been held over the years – plot the different host cities on a map of the world. Do you know the country in which each city may be found?

Art Games

The symbol for the Olympic Games is five interlocking rings. Try to think of a brand new symbol that could be used to represent the today. Try out lots of designs in a sketch-book, and write about each one, stating the pros and cons of the design. You will need to consider what the Games are about – what do they stand for? What is their greatest achievement?

Story

Write a story in which the Olympic Games comes to your city. Describe the preparation that is carried out prior to the Games – perhaps focusing on one particular new stadium and describing how magical it is. Think carefully about who your main characters are – and the viewpoints they hold. Will you include some opposing views in the story to create drama? Perhaps not everyone wanted the Games to happen.

Section 3: Curriculum Overview

Curriculum Overview	National Curriculum references
PSHE and Citizenship	1a, 2a, 2d, 2f, 2j, 2k, 4a, 5a, 5c-e,
English	En1: 2a, 2d, 2e, 3a-e, 4a; En2: 3a, 3e-g, 5b-c, 5f, 9a-c; En3: 1a-e, 2a-c, 3, 7c, 9c, 9d, 10, 12
NLS Text Types	chronological reports and recounts visual recount (timeline) annotated visual reports stories.
Geography	1a-e, 2c, 3b, 3g, 5a, 6d, 7a-b
History	1a-b, 4a, 4b, 5a-c, 6, 7
Art and Design	1b, 1c, 3a-b, 4a
ICT	1a, 1b, 3a, 5a, 5b

Context Builder 6	Unit 6 (Year 6)

Context   Your city has beaten its rivals to become the nation's main bid to host a future Olympic Games. If the city is chosen by the International Olympic Committee (IOC) then a major building programme would be necessary, costing the city, and the nation, many millions of pounds – but the fame and notoriety gained from staging this world class event may be worth it. Opinion is divided.

Scenario   Preparing for the Games would bring new jobs, new sports facilities, new transport systems and so on. The gain in tourism too, as the world's media turns its spotlight towards the city, would be significant. Nevertheless, not everyone is backing the bid with some believing that the cost of staging this major event would mean other more urgent and deserving causes within the city, such as hospitals, education and housing would be neglected.

Glossary   *Olympic Games* – a sports competition in which many countries of the world come together to compete in many different events.

Bid – a submission to the Olympic International Committee to stage the Olympic Games in the city.

Character Card: For | Unit 6 (Year 6)

The following characters support the city's Olympic bid:

Recommended characters:

- member of tourist board
- parent with young children
- hotel owner
- sports coach
- headteacher of local comprehensive school.

Further suggestions:

transport worker

local MP (Member of Parliament)

unemployed resident

manager of local swimming club

representative from the chamber of commerce.

Character Card: Against | Unit 6 (Year 6)

The following characters oppose the Olympic bid:

Recommended characters:

- housing officer
- local resident
- hospital manager
- local commuter
- theatre director.

Further suggestions:

road safety officer

resident of rival city

wildlife campaigner

local resident

schools inspector.

Character Profile 1: Member of tourist board

When the Olympic Games comes to a city, so too does the world's attention. The giant media spotlight shines on its streets and buildings for two whole weeks. Get the coverage right and you've got a two-week long advertisement for the city, with all its attractions. History shows that in the weeks and months that follow an Olympic Games, there is a great rise in tourists visiting the host city. As a tourist officer you are sure that putting the city 'on the map' in this way could be a very good thing indeed.

Character Profile 2: Parent with young children

If and when the Olympics comes to your city, your children will be old enough to take a real interest in sport. The unique opportunity of seeing athletes from all over the world compete at the very highest level will inspire and enthuse your children and, who knows, they may go on to be the gold medal winners of the future! The Games will certainly help many young people in the city to see the importance and enjoyment in leading fit and healthy lives. Do something special for the children: bring the Olympic flame to town!

Character Profile 3: Hotel owner

When you heard of the bid to host the Games in your city, straight away you saw the possible boost in trade for you and all the other hoteliers in the area. Business is slower now than in recent years, with many tourists choosing to visit other places here and abroad rather than come to holiday in your city. The Games could provide some much needed income for so many people in the area – and just think, you might even have some famous guests signing your visitors' book!

Character Profile 4: Sports coach

Inspiring and coaching young sportsmen and sportswomen is your business; what better way then to show them how to succeed than by bringing the sporting heroes of the world into their own neighbourhood? Another major benefit of hosting the Games is the legacy of sport and leisure facilities that will be left behind when the athletes have gone and the world's media have turned to the next Olympics. From training grounds and pools to full-scale stadiums – the city will be a centre of excellence for sport.

Character Profile 5: Headteacher of local comprehensive school

As a school that is trying to develop a reputation for excellence in sport, this news is just what you need to inspire your pupils to don their running shoes and break some records! You can just picture the trips you shall organise to take children to the major events, many of which will literally be just down the road. Who knows, you may even be playing host to some competitors on your new, state of the art astro-turf!

Character Profile 6: Housing officer

All this talk of Olympic Games may sound exciting to many, but some people are forgetting just how much the event will cost to host. The many millions of pounds that would need to be set aside to prepare for the Games could, and should in your view, be spent on other much more urgent needs within the city. Many residents are living in council housing that is below acceptable standards – and there are hundreds more on waiting lists for further accommodation. You worry that the city's housing problem will be ignored when the money is used to build fancy stadiums and Olympic villages.

Character Profile 7: Local resident

As a local resident in the city centre, you have seen a massive rise in traffic and pedestrians over the last few years, with the city reaching bursting point. More and more people are coming to work in the city and you are worried that soon life in the city centre will be intolerable. There is nowhere to park, all the shops and restaurants are permanently full and the cinemas are booked out until next month. All good news for businesses, but you are rapidly feeling like a sardine in a can. And now, just when the city's infrastructure is fit to burst, you hear talk of hosting an Olympic Games! Just where exactly?

Character Profile 8: Hospital manager

You are worried that the excitement over the Olympic Games coming to town would overshadow a very real problem in the city, that is, one of declining standards in health care due to poor investment. In other words, you need more money poured into your hospital to improve the level of service you can provide. The millions of pounds that will have to be spent in preparing the city's sports facilities, could be used to improve so many aspects of hospitals and the emergency services, ultimately saving lives.

Character Profile 9: Local commuter

Olympics? Are you serious? Just where would the hundreds of thousands of visitors park? Isn't traffic congestion bad enough at the moment without doubling the number of cars on the road? It currently takes you over an hour to get from the suburbs into your office in the city centre. Just imagine how much chaos there will be on the roads when the world's sporting fans arrive. The Olympics is a wonderful event, and you would love to see it in this country, but there are larger cities around, none of which have the crazy one way systems and giant roundabouts that you have! The city's roads just couldn't take the pressure!

Character Profile 10: Theatre director

Why does this country have such an obsession with sport? You enjoy a good game of tennis every now and again, and watching England play on the TV but millions of pounds to build yet more stadiums and athletics tracks? The city is badly in need of some new theatres and arts complexes. Isn't it about time we started providing for the young painters and actors of the future? You had the chance to host an International Music Festival in the city last year, but the council turned it down, saying they could not afford it! And now the Olympics?

Character Record Sheet

Name.....................................

Pupil name:
Character role:
Views:

Pupil name:
Character role:
Views:

Pupil name:
Character role:
Views:

Pupil name:
Character role:
Views:

Pupil name:
Character role:
Views:

The Curtain Falls

Section 1: Lesson Plans

Lesson 1

Set up a circle meeting in class. Introduce the theme for the unit by reading out the following Context Builder 7 (also enclosed at the end of the unit).

Context Builder 7	Unit 7 (Year 7)

Context	A new headteacher, Mrs Jacobs, has arrived at Greenwood Comprehensive. She has stated that her first priority is to close down the aging dance and drama studio and replace it with a state of the art ICT suite, with twenty computers, interactive white boards, projectors and conference facilities. Mrs Jacobs' plan is to turn Greenwood into a centre for excellence in ICT. Dance and drama will continue to be taught, but in the multi-purpose gymnasium. To have both a studio and an ICT suite would be nice – but the school budget will not stretch that far.
Scenario	Many of the governors, parents, staff and pupils are excited about the new plan, believing as they do that modern computer technology will enhance learning right across the curriculum. However, there are others in the Greenwood community who worry that the creative arts, including dance and drama are becoming sidelined, receiving less and less funding and attention. They say, computers may be useful in life, but expressing yourself through dance and drama makes life worth living!
Glossary	*ICT* – Information and Communications Technology *Fringe* – outside mainstream practice, unconventional.

Elicit pupils' initial thoughts about the role of ICT in today's learning. How important is it that schools stay up to date with technological advances?

Broaden the discussion to consider the role of comprehensive schools generally in preparing their students for working life. What are the key professional skills they will need? Where does computer literacy fit into that? In what way does ICT impact on the rest of the curriculum?

Consider the arts – focusing on dance and drama in particular. Invite the children to share their ideas on the role such pursuits play in the children's general education. Should they enjoy the same attention and funding as ICT? In what ways do the performing arts impact on the curriculum generally?

Think about who might support and who might oppose Mrs Jacobs' plan to replace the studio with an ICT suite and move the dance and drama classes to the gymnasium.

When everyone has had the chance to contribute, establish the groups for the unit. You may wish to record the names in each group for future lessons. Then read out the following Character Cards, (also enclosed at the end of the unit), and give each pupil a role to play.

Character Card: For	Unit 7 (Year 7)

The following characters support the plan to replace the studio with an ICT suite:

Recommended characters:

- ICT coordinator
- parent of Year 7 pupil
- governor (and ICT specialist)
- parent (and local business manager)
- french teacher.

Further suggestions:

Year 11 pupil (member of school council)

school secretary

Science teacher

governor (and college lecturer)

school careers advisor.

Character Card: Against	Unit 7 (Year 7)

The following characters oppose the plan to replace the dance and drama studio:

Recommended characters:

- parent of Year 8 pupil
- dance teacher
- governor (and recruitment advisor)
- English teacher
- PE coordinator.

Further suggestions:

Year 9 pupil (member of school council)

County arts officer

parent (and ex-dancer)

art teacher

grandparent of pupil (and theatre director).

Individual Character Profiles (enclosed at the end of the unit) will offer each participant a brief summary of his or her character's viewpoint in relation to the scenario – that is, how and why they will be affected by the outcome.

There are a total of ten characters available (five recommended characters from each side), though others may be added if necessary. All pupils in each group must receive a different role – and preferably half the roles will come from Character Card: For and the other half from Character Card Against.

Explain to the pupils what is to happen next: before the next workshop (Lesson 2), the pupils must spend time developing opinions and constructing arguments in bullet points, on behalf of their character. Each pupil will need to come to the group ready to support or oppose the plan to replace the studio with an ICT suite. They will need to consider how the decision will impact on their character, but also on how they can put forward arguments that refer to the needs of others too. The most successful arguments will be those that consider the greatest number of people (rather than just an individual's own needs), and those that reflect the roles of ICT and the performing arts in the curriculum generally.

Lesson 2

Begin with a circle meeting. Revisit the vision statement, core values and group pledges of the preliminary lessons. Reiterate the importance of abiding by the pledges when interacting within the group discussions that follow. Everyone must have a chance to speak and to listen.

The pupils reform the groups from Lesson 1. Give a copy of the Character Record Sheet to every pupil. Each group member will have a turn to share their views on the plan for the proposed ICT suite. Pupils will need to listen carefully to each others' ideas, noting down the names, roles and a brief two-line summary of the views of the other members in their group. Collect in the record sheets at the end of the session – and check against the original Character Profile cards.

At the end of the session, hold a short plenary in which children are invited to report back to the whole class not on their specific views and arguments, but on the process of sharing opinions – was it helpful to find others with similar views? Was there a sense of different sides forming in the group as people discovered who shared their own views and who did not? Which was easier, expressing one's own viewpoint or listening to the views of another? Did the children find themselves paying more attention to those who shared similar views to their own?

Explain to the pupils the next step in the unit. They are to prepare a paper (can take the form of a persuasive pamphlet) or a poster, that promotes the role of ICT or Dance and Drama in the curriculum, thereby supporting or opposing the plans for the studio. The pamphlet or posters would be distributed amongst the school community to build support for either viewpoint. Their work will need to be visually appealing, as well as informative and concise.

The next workshop will be a general meeting hosted by the Chair of school governors (the teacher) in which the views of the different members of the Greenwood School community will be heard, before final options are presented and a democratic vote takes place to decide the course of action. In this session, pupils will be able to refer to both the bullet points from Lesson 1 and the pamphlets or posters in from this session.

Lesson 3

The lesson begins with a short group session in which pupils who are playing the same characters across the groups get together to share ideas and thoughts, and prepare a good argument in favour or opposing the plan to create the new ICT suite in place of the drama studio. They can refer to their bullet points or pamphlets and posters for their views if they wish. Each group of 'like-characters' will need to elect a spokesperson (someone different from the spokesperson for Unit 6). The elected speaker will address the class at the following public meeting.

Come together as a class and explain the procedure for the public meeting: there will be a table at the front of the room from which the Chair of Governors (the teacher) will host the meeting. Sitting either side of the Chairperson will be the elected spokespersons (one of every recommended character from the character cards, that is, five on each side). The format for the meeting can be altered to suit timings and location, but a suggested order might be:

- Chairperson (the teacher) opens the meeting by introducing the plan to create a state of the art ICT suite on the site of the old drama studio, and to re-house all dance and drama lessons in the multi-purpose gymnasium, also on the school site.

- Chairperson invites each of the characters to present their viewpoints, beginning with someone in favour of the plan and then alternating between those who agree and those who disagree.

- Chairperson invites comments from the floor – this is an opportunity for other pupils to ask questions or express their views.

- Final vote – for this you will need to distil the different ideas into a shortlist of options. These might include:

  1. Go ahead with the plan to replace the studio with the ICT suite and re-house all dance and drama lessons in the gym.

  2. Keep the studio as it is and find an alternative existing site to recreate as an ICT suite (simply building a new one from scratch is not an option, due to lack of funds and site space).

  3. Upgrade the studio to a more modern facility, distribute the new ICT resources around the school.

Once the options have been established – all pupils vote for the one they would settle for.

The different characters may well have different views – and it was very important that these were properly heard. However, once the options are listed, pupils will need to consider the question:

If I cannot have exactly what I want, what would the next best thing be?

Lesson 4

This shorter session comprises of a class discussion (out of role), in which all pupils may feedback to the rest of the group their thoughts on the role play. The meeting can be an informal discussion loosely based around the themes of tolerance, empathy and cooperation, or you may wish to lead the session using the following questions as a guide:

- How can one decide which is more important – the arts or ICT?

- Why do such dilemmas arise? Discuss notion of limited funds to spend, so a need to prioritise.

- Can a curriculum ever keep everyone happy all the time? How important is it to appeal to a broad range of skills and interest?

- Should we be prescribing what is or is not important in children's lives? If so, where do we start?

Section 2: Follow-up Activities

Maths project

Using the internet, magazines and catalogues, invite the children to find out more about the cost of furnishing a new ICT suite. You may wish to set the pupils a budget and ask them to see what sort of ICT suite they can design, with what resources. They will need to present their ideas as a spending plan – with details of the items they would buy and their prices.

Newspaper Report

The plan to create a brand new ICT facility at Greenwood Comprehensive School has been approved and the suite is nearing completion. As a journalist with the local newspaper, you have been invited along to the grand opening of the building. Write a feature for your paper, in which you describe the new facility at Greenwood. You may wish to include within your piece a reference to the mixed opinions in the community about the plan to re-house the dance and drama activities elsewhere. Remember to include interviews with staff, parents and pupils.

Geography

How do schools, or private residents, obtain permission to build or extend their properties? Who needs to know when land is about to be used for a different purpose? Why do you think others need to know? Conduct a study investigating what is involved when a person wishes to make alterations to their property. Write an explanation text, explaining the process (in basic terms) and then explain why you think it is important to place restrictions on building plans.

Debate Speech

Write a debate speech either proposing or opposing the following motion:

This House believes that to be computer literate is more important than being able to dance or act; ICT in schools deserves more time and money than any individual creative subject.

Section 3: Curriculum Overview

Curriculum Overview	National Curriculum references
Citizenship (KS3)	1g, 2a-c, 3a-c
English	En1: 1a, 2b-c, 3a-e, 4a, 8a-b ; En2: 1d, 3a-b, 4b-c, 9a-b ; En3: 1e-f, 1i-m, 9b-d1a-e, 10.
NLS Text Types	chronological reports and recounts visual recount (timeline) annotated visual reports stories.
Geography	1a-e, 2c, 3b, 3g, 5a, 6d, 7a-b
History	1a-b, 4a, 4b, 5a-c, 6, 7
Art and Design	1b, 1c, 3a-b, 4a
ICT	1a, 1b, 3a, 5a, 5b.

Context Builder 7	Unit 7 (Year 7)

Context A new headteacher, Mrs Jacobs, has arrived at Greenwood Comprehensive. She has stated that her first priority is to close down the aging dance and drama studio and replace it with a state of the art ICT suite, with twenty computers, interactive white boards, projectors and conference facilities. Mrs Jacobs' plan is to turn Greenwood into a centre for excellence in ICT. Dance and drama will continue to be taught, but in the multi-purpose gymnasium. To have both a studio and an ICT suite would be nice – but the school budget will not stretch that far.

Scenario Many of the governors, parents, staff and pupils are excited about the new plan, believing as they do that modern computer technology will enhance learning right across the curriculum. However, there are others in the Greenwood community who worry that the creative arts, including dance and drama are becoming sidelined, receiving less and less funding and attention. They say, computers may be useful in life, but expressing yourself through dance and drama makes life worth living!

Glossary *ICT* – Information and Communications Technology

Fringe – outside mainstream practice, unconventional.

Character Card: For   Unit 7 (Year 7)

The following characters support the plan to replace the studio with an ICT suite:

Recommended characters:

- ICT coordinator
- parent of Year 7 pupil
- governor (and ICT specialist)
- parent (and local business manager)
- french teacher.

Further suggestions:

Year 11 pupil (member of school council)

school secretary

science teacher

governor (and college lecturer)

school careers advisor.

Character Card: Against   Unit 7 (Year 7)

The following characters oppose the plan to replace the dance and drama studio:

Recommended characters:

- parent of Year 8 pupil
- dance teacher
- governor (and recruitment advisor)
- English teacher
- PE coordinator.

Further suggestions:

Year 9 pupil (member of school council)

county arts officer

parent (and ex-dancer)

art teacher

grandparent of pupil (and theatre director).

Character Profile 1: ICT coordinator

The proposed ICT suite presents a unique opportunity to bring the most modern technology into the curriculum, benefiting all subjects, from French to History. The suite will be open to all members of staff to book times in it with their classes, and take advantage of the many different ICT packages that will help learning in their own subjects. How could anyone refuse it? As the ICT coordinator, you have the knowledge and, more importantly, the will, to devote much of your time to building a first-class resource that the school can be proud of.

Character Profile 2: Parent of Year 7 pupil

One of the few subjects in the curriculum that interests your son is ICT. He struggles in many other areas at school and often seems disinterested and apathetic, yet when he returns home he turns straight to his computer and creates the most magical programmes and presentations. He has a real flair for computer technology and, given the right support from school, will go far. The proposed ICT suite is just what your son needs to get him interested in school and, hopefully, in learning generally.

Character Profile 3: Governor (and ICT specialist)

You have said for some time now that the school's ICT resources are behind the times. With old PCs and very few interactive white boards in the school, Greenwood is in danger of falling behind many of its rival schools. Besides, developing children's ICT skills will give them the proper start they need in the age of global communications technology. The proposed ICT suite is exactly what you have been calling for – and you are well placed to offer the school free advice on how to get the best deals and the best service around.

Character Profile 4: Parent (and local business manager)

As a successful business manager you recruit many employees each year and the most important thing you look for in new staff is a good level of computer literacy. Global communications are at the centre of many businesses, and schools must keep up with the pace of changes in technology if their pupils are to secure good jobs in the modern world.

The proposed ICT suite would certainly go a long way in equipping children with the right skills and experience that would unlock so many doors in the future. Businesses of all kinds would be interested in the plan – and perhaps would offer some sponsorship too.

Character Profile 5: French teacher

As a modern languages teacher you are always on the look out for new ways of developing pupils' language ability in exciting and interactive ways. There are so many ICT based packages out there that would greatly assist your teaching. You would certainly be queuing up to book lessons in the new ICT suite – and make French an exciting and modern learning experience for all pupils.

Character Profile 6: Parent of Year 8 pupil

Your daughter has really thrived since starting at Greenwood, and this is due in no small measure to the opportunities she has had for developing her drama and dance. She is a very creative child who loves expressing her self through the arts. Though her academic skills are progressing well, it is frequent visits to the arts studio that make her days worthwhile. If the studio goes, you are worried that her enjoyment in school will go with it – and a dip in enthusiasm now could mean bad news for other subjects too.

Character Profile 7: Dance teacher

Watching the children flourish as they find confidence and self-esteem through dance and drama has been rewarding for you. Many parents have commented that their sons or daughters always seem happier at home and at school when they are working on a dance or rehearsing lines for a play. Though you have been offered slots in the multi-purpose gym to continue teaching dance, you fear that the children will feel less inclined to take part.

Character Profile 8: Governor (and recruitment consultant)

As a professional recruitment consultant, and governor, you have a wealth of experience in interviewing people, trying to match the right staff to the right jobs. You are sure that one of the most important things employers look for in any interview is confidence and enthusiasm – in abundance! Creative subjects in school, like dance and drama, have an important role in building children's confidence and bringing a sense of fun and excitement, raising children's enthusiasm for learning. There is nothing to beat an enthusiastic smile and a creative mind in an interview situation. The show must go on!

Character Profile 9: English teacher

As the school's Head of English, you see dance and drama as very useful ways of improving pupils' love of books and storytelling generally. You have often used the studio to run dramatic activities based on various class books you are teaching. Participating in dramatic productions of all kinds certainly helps pupils' language skills in many ways, improving their speaking skills, building empathy with fictional characters and so on. In some ways the drama studio is an extension of your classroom – an exciting arena in which books can be explored and stories can be told together. You feel that active role-playing has to be better than staring at a computer screen, hasn't it?

Character Profile 10: PE coordinator

You welcome the idea of improving the school's ICT resources, although you feel frustrated that it has to be at the expense of dance – a subject that helps children to become fitter and stronger. Also, the new plan to re-house dance and drama lessons in the gymnasium spells trouble for your PE lessons, particularly when there is a school production on the go and rehearsals are coming thick and fast. There are only so many hours in the day and only one gymnasium to spend them in! As much as you like the creative subjects, you cannot have them disturbing your own lessons. Surely the studio should stay?

Character Record Sheet

Name...................................

Pupil name:	
Character role:	
Views:	

Pupil name:	
Character role:	
Views:	

Pupil name:	
Character role:	
Views:	

Pupil name:	
Character role:	
Views:	

Pupil name:	
Character role:	
Views:	

Brookwood Motors Inc.

Section 1: Lesson Plans

Lesson 1

Arrange a circle meeting for the whole class. Introduce the theme for the unit by reading out the following Context Builder 8 (included at the end of this unit, for photocopying purposes).

Context Builder 8	Unit 8 (Year 7)
Context	In a small, semi-rural town in the north east of England, the local council has received a planning application from a large multi-national car manufacturer, Brookwood Motors Inc., to build a new factory plant on the outskirts of the town.
Scenario	The new site will bring hundreds of jobs to an area that sees low employment and will bring some much needed business to local shopkeepers and tradesmen. However, the proposed site is a stretch of common land, currently used by the town's residents for sporting and recreational pursuits. The planning application has aroused much interest, and controversy, in the area. Letters appear in newspapers, petitions are gathered and even protests are staged until a public meeting is called.
Glossary	*Council* – a group of local officials who govern the area. *Planning Application* – a request to the council for permission to build or extend a property or premises.

Engage the children in a discussion of who in the community might be affected by the proposed plans. Encourage pupils to see the issue from both sides: its benefits and its drawbacks. Invite any children who have experienced similar situations in their own localities to share their observations and feelings.

Discuss with the group how interested parties might go about making their views known (letters, petitions, protests, meetings etc.) Initiate a discussion about the importance of respecting other people's views and responding to others' ideas sensitively and appropriately. Encourage the group to see the importance of finding solutions and compromises which keep the greatest number of people happy.

When everyone has had the chance to contribute, read out the following Character Cards (also enclosed at the end of the unit for photocopying), and give each pupil a role to play.

Character Card: For   Unit 8 (Year 7)

The following characters support the plan to replace the studio with an ICT suite:

Recommended characters:

- headteacher of local primary school
- manager of local Job Centre
- local shopkeeper
- local builder
- local police officer.

Further suggestions:

chairman of local Chamber of Commerce

town Mayor

owner of nearby petrol station

careers advisor in local secondary school

youth leader.

Character Card: Against   Unit 8 (Year 7)

The following characters are against the plan to build the car plant:

Recommended characters:

- representative from the Royal Society for the Protection of Birds.
- local resident with teenage children
- football coach
- member of local Ramblers' Association
- local dog walker.

Further suggestions:

headteacher of local secondary school

local road user

council representative for the Green Party

representative from the Scout Movement.

Individual Character Profiles (at the end of the unit) will offer each pupil a brief summary of his or her character's viewpoint in relation to the scenario – that is, how and why they will be affected by the outcome.

There are a total of ten characters available (five recommended characters from each side), though others may be added if necessary. All pupils in each group must receive a different role – and preferably half the roles will come from Character Card: For and the other half from Character Card Against.

Explain to the pupils what is to happen next. Before the next workshop (Lesson 2), the pupils must spend time developing opinions and constructing arguments in bullet points, on behalf of their character. Each pupil will need to come to the group ready to support the plan to build the car factory or to argue against it, with good reasons in support. They will need to consider how the decision will impact on their character, but also on how they can put forward arguments that refer to the needs of others too. The most successful arguments will be those that consider the greatest number of people (rather than just an individual character's own needs).

During the intervening period between lessons, (this may be a day or a week, depending on your timetable), you may wish to invite children to seek your help if they encounter problems in finding ideas for their character.

Lesson 2

Begin with a circle meeting. Revisit the vision statement, core values and group pledges of the preliminary lessons. Reiterate the importance of abiding by the pledges when interacting within the group discussions that follow. Everyone must have a chance to speak and to listen.

The pupils reform the groups from Lesson 1. Give a copy of the Character Record Sheet. Each group member will have a turn to share their views on the plan to build the Brookwood Car Plant. Pupils will need to listen carefully to each others' ideas, noting down the names, roles and a brief two-line summary of the views of the other members in their group. Collect in the record sheets at the end of the session – and check against the original Character Profile cards.

At the end of the session, hold a short plenary in which children are invited to report back to the whole class not on their specific views and arguments, but on the process of sharing opinions – was it helpful to find others with similar views? Was there a sense of different sides forming in the group as people discovered who shared their own views and who did not? Which was easier, expressing one's own viewpoint or listening to the views of another? Did the children find themselves paying more attention to those who shared similar views to their own?

Explain to the pupils the next step in the unit – each pupil is to prepare a formal letter to the local council, either supporting the plan to build the factory or opposing it, with good reasons in support. The next workshop will be a general meeting hosted by the Chairperson of the local council (that is, the teacher) in which the bullet points and notes from Lesson 1 and the formal letters from this lesson can be referred to when characters come to defend their views.

Lesson 3

At the beginning of the lesson hold a short group session in which pupils who are playing the same characters across the groups get together to share ideas and thoughts, and prepare a good argument in favour or opposing the new plans for the Brookwood Factory. They can refer to their bullet points or letters for their views if they wish. Each group of 'like-characters' will need to elect a spokesperson (some one different from the spokesperson for Unit 7). The elected speaker will address the class at the following public meeting.

Come together as a class and explain the procedure for the public meeting: there will be a table at the front of the room from which the Chairperson (the teacher) will host the meeting. Sitting either side of the Chairperson will be the elected spokespersons (one of every recommended character from the character cards: five on each side). The format for the meeting can be altered to suit timings and location, but a suggested order might be:

- Chairperson (the teacher) opens the meeting by explaining the plans to build the car plant on the common land.

- Chairperson invites each of the characters to present their viewpoints, beginning with someone in favour of building the car factory then alternating between those who agree and those who disagree.

- Chairperson invites comments from the floor – this is an opportunity for other pupils to ask questions or express their views.

- Final vote – for this you will need to distil the different ideas into a shortlist of options. These might include:

  1. Go ahead with the plan to build the Brookwood Car Factory.

  2. Build the car factory on the proposed site, but set up a new recreation ground on an alternative site for the local residents to use instead of the original common.

  3. Find a different site for the Brookwood Car Plant in the local area, and retain the common.

  4. Retain the common and find a site for the factory in another part of the country altogether.

Once the options have been established – all pupils vote for the one they would settle for.

The different characters may well have different views – and it was very important that these were properly heard. However, once the options are listed, pupils will need to consider the question:

If I cannot have exactly what I want, what would the next best thing be?

Lesson 4

This shorter session comprises of a class discussion (out of role), in which all pupils may feedback to the rest of the group their thoughts on the role-play. The meeting can be an informal discussion loosely based around the themes of tolerance, empathy and cooperation, or you may wish to lead the session using the following questions as a guide:

- Which was more important do you think, jobs or recreational needs?

- How might a council reach a planning decision in real life? How would they canvass people's opinions?

- Did the process of deciding seem more complicated as you heard other people's viewpoints?

- Which of the options would keep the most people satisfied in the long run?

- Do you think Brookwood Motors INC. has a duty to the local community? Should it contribute to a new recreation ground? If so, why should it?

Section 2: Follow-up Activities

Newspaper Articles

Ask the pupils to bring in recent editions of tabloid and broadsheet newspapers. Compare styles, focusing upon language, format, artwork and authorial voice. Explain to the class that they must write their own newspaper articles (journalistic recounts) that tell the story of the controversy over the Brookwood factory. They will need to write two articles, one in a broadsheet style (for example, The Times) and the other in a tabloid style (for example, The Mirror).

Local History Study

Investigate how a locality was affected by a significant local development this is taken from the NC Programme of Study for History, point 7.

Examples might include the introduction or closure of a large industry in the area and its effects on the local population. Using primary and secondary sources, pupils investigate how the changes affected the lives of the local people (for example, the closing of a pit, the building of a large retail park).

Fieldwork

Choosing a local site, pupils propose a hypothetical plan to change the use of the land (for example, to build a supermarket, factory or school). Invite the pupils to consider the environmental implications of such a change, including increased traffic congestion, hedgerow loss, increased demand on resources. Pupils should consider the wider aspects of how settlements evolve through such changes in land use and the need to manage environments sustainably. Remind pupils that the health of the environment depends upon the successful collaboration of its inhabitants in resolving issues and reaching ecologically sound compromises.

Design Brief

Divide the class into small working groups of three or four. Each group must come up with a design for the new factory. Using a combination of profile and aerial views, the groups must settle on an agreed design, which is aesthetically tolerable, ecologically sound and financially viable (perhaps the designers could work to a given budget). All group members should produce designs in the early stages and the final design should be one which is acceptable to the whole group.

Prose or Poem

Imagine you are visiting the old common, early in the morning, perhaps to walk your dog or go for a run (as an adult, rather than on your own as a child!). Try to describe the sights, sounds and smells of the place in the early morning mist. What does it feel like to be somewhere so quiet, before the hustle bustle of the working day commences? Remember to include some interesting adjectives, adverbs, similes and metaphors to bring your piece to life for the reader.

Section 3: Curriculum Overview

Curriculum Overview	National Curriculum references
Citizenship (KS3)	1g-i, 2a, 2b, 3a-c
English	En1: 1-7, 10, 11a; En2: 1d, 4a-d, En3: 1b-c, 1i-n, 2a, 4b-d, 7c-e, 9b-c.
NLS Text Types	persuasive: letters, leaflets, speeches informative: public notices, articles journalistic: newspaper reports fiction: prose or poems.
Geography	1d-e, 3g, 4b, 5a, 6a, 6d
History	4a-b, 7
Art and Design	1a, 2c, 3b, 5b-d
ICT	2a, 3b, 4a-c, 5a-b
Design and technology	1a-d, 3a, 3c.

Context Builder 8	Unit 8 (Year 7)

Context

In a small, semi-rural town in the north east of England, the local council has received a planning application from a large multi-national car manufacturer, Brookwood Motors Inc., to build a new factory plant on the outskirts of the town.

Scenario

The new site will bring hundreds of jobs to an area that sees low employment and will bring some much needed business to local shopkeepers and tradesmen. However, the proposed site is a stretch of common land, currently used by the town's residents for sporting and recreational pursuits. The planning application has aroused much interest, and controversy, in the area. Letters appear in newspapers, petitions are gathered and even protests are staged until a public meeting is called.

Glossary

Council – a group of local officials who govern the area.

Planning Application – a request to the council for permission to build or extend a property or premises.

Character Card: For   Unit 8 (Year 7)

The following characters support the plan to replace the studio with an ICT suite:

Recommended characters:

- head teacher of local primary school
- manager of local Job Centre
- local shopkeeper
- local builder
- local police officer.

Further suggestions:

chairman of local Chamber of Commerce

town Mayor

owner of nearby petrol station

careers advisor in local secondary school

youth leader.

Character Card: Against   Unit 8 (Year 7)

The following characters are against the plan to build the car plant:

Recommended characters:

- representative from the Royal Society for the Protection of Birds.
- local resident with teenage children
- football coach
- member of local Ramblers' Association
- local dog walker.

Further suggestions:

head teacher of local secondary school

local road user

council representative for the Green Party

representative from the Scout Movement.

Character Profile 1: headteacher of local primary school

Numbers on roll have certainly dipped in the last few years, reflecting the town's falling number of residents as people are forced to look elsewhere for employment. The local education authority has begun to talk of merging schools together. Building the car plant so close to the school would certainly mean many more people moving to the area – and this would inevitably mean more pupils for your school. Brookwood Motors could be the good news you have been hoping for.

Character Profile 2: Manager of local Job Centre

For some time now you have had many more applicants than actual positions to fill and this is causing much frustration and anger in the visitors that come through your doors each day. You would like to help them all, but if the jobs aren't out there, you're are helpless. The proposed plan to build the car plant would mean hundreds of new jobs and many more smiling faces. It simply must go ahead.

Character Profile 3: Local shopkeeper

More workers in the area, all travelling to and from the Brookwood car plant, all stopping at your shop for a newspaper and a sandwich? It sounds the perfect remedy for a local business that has been dwindling of late and will soon be threatened with closure if profits don't rise. There are many local shopkeepers like you who have seen a loss of business since the giant supermarkets came to town. This new plan would potentially save a great many shops in the local area; it must go ahead.

Character Profile 4: Local builder

As a local builder you rely heavily on word of mouth recommendations from local residents. Over the last few years, you have seen many people leave the area in search of employment and this has meant fewer building contracts for you. The plan to build the car factory would mean hundreds more residents coming into the area and, in turn, this would eventually mean more building jobs for you. With a growing family it is vital that you can earn enough money to live on – and if things don't pick up soon, you will have no choice but to leave the area.

Character Profile 5: Local police officer

You are worried that the lack of jobs for local residents, particularly young adults leaving school, is having an impact on the number of reported petty crimes in the area as youths leave school only to face a life of loitering around on street corners, getting up to mischief. When young people feel that society does not need them, they soon feel disinclined to obey its rules. The new car plant could be just what the local community needs to get its young people off the streets and earning a decent wage.

Character Profile 6: Representative from the RSPB

Local joggers and dog walkers are not the only land-users who might be affected by the plan to build a car factory on the common, the land is currently home to a great many species of wildlife too. Birds of many kinds nest in the area, which is a peaceful haven away from the busy suburbs and cities that make up the north east conurbation. To lose the common would mean losing yet more native and migrant birds – it must not be allowed to happen.

Character Profile 7: Local resident with teenage children

Your two teenage children virtually live up on the common! Every weekend, and after school in the spring and summer, they can be found playing football with friends or simply relaxing in the fields, enjoying the fresh air (and the privacy away from mum and dad!). To lose the land might mean jobs for them in the future – but try telling that to them on a Saturday morning when they have nowhere to go and play. You are worried that when teenagers have their only source of amusement removed from them, they face an uncertain future of loitering around on street corners, feeling disinclined to behave.

Character Profile 8: Football coach

The area of land that is proposed for the car factory currently plays to host to a dozen football teams, all sharing its fields to train and meet up for Sunday league matches. It is a lifeline for your club and you do not fancy the prospect of telling your teenage players that the team will have to fold if they lose their only place to play. The faces of the players and the sound of the crowds of supporters cheering each Sunday remind you that this particular area of town is a very cherished one for a lot of people. The health, fitness and happiness of so many residents would be affected by this plan.

Character Profile 9: Member of local Ramblers' Association

There are many footpaths that dissect the stretch of common land currently proposed for the car factory. Many of your fellow walkers can be found up at the common each weekend, enjoying the wildlife and a good walk. Building the giant car plant would mean so many important footpaths would disappear, or be redirected. And who wants to walk right next to a car factory anyway? There are few areas of natural beauty left in the area as it is, without losing one more.

Character Profile 10: Local dog walker

Early morning walks have become an integral part of your day, as you set off with your dog before work, for a few treasured moments of peace and quiet. You often pass other dog walkers and joggers who smile politely as they too grab some precious peace before starting the working day. There are so few other green areas nearby that you simply don't know what you will do if the factory is built.

Character Record Sheet   Name.....................................

Pupil name:
Character role:
Views:

Pupil name:
Character role:
Views:

Pupil name:
Character role:
Views:

Pupil name:
Character role:
Views:

Pupil name:
Character role:
Views:

Star Struck

Section 1: Lesson Plans

Lesson 1

Arrange a circle meeting for the whole class. Introduce the theme for the unit by reading out Context Builder 9 (enclosed at the end of this unit, for photocopying purposes).

Context Builder 9	Unit 9 (Year 7)
Context	A controversial space programme is planned for the country. With a space centre and launch site to rival the USA's Kennedy Space Centre and Cape Canaveral, the nation will become a major player in the race to put an astronaut on Mars... but many feel there are other more worthy needs on Earth.
Scenario	The Government has arranged a series of cluster meetings, or 'focus groups' across the country, in which members of the public are invited to share their views in response to the proposed plan to build the new space centre. One such focus group takes place in the following unit, in which very different viewpoints are revealed.
Glossary	*Controversial* – open to question; disputable or debatable. *Cluster* – a gathering or group. *Worthy* – deserving; admirable; worthwhile.

Elicit pupils' initial thoughts about space travel and consider its role in our culture. How popular is science fiction? How often does fiction become reality? What is it about exploring space that so captures our imagination? Does it really matter to us here on Earth?

Consider the benefits of having our own space centre. Why would it be beneficial to the country? What could space travel give us? Is it important to reach beyond the stars and see what lies out there? Can the children think of how space exploration impacts on the daily lives of ordinary people on Earth? Consider advances in medicine, science, evolution etc. Are there lessons we could learn from the atmospheres and composition of other planets? What if there is life out there?

Consider other, more political, reasons why it might be good for a country to boast its own space programme. Does it inspire confidence in others across the world? Would people regard our country differently if we joined the 'space race'?

Then consider any objections that people might make to the proposed space programme. Is it all about priorities? What other priorities should a nation, and its government, have when deciding how to spend public money? Building and maintaining a space programme is one of the most, if not the most, expensive project for any nation. Is it worth all the money, or are there other more worthy causes here on Earth? Would some people feel more strongly about this than others?

When everyone has had the chance to contribute, establish the groups for the unit. You may wish to record the names in each group for future lessons. Then read out the following Character Cards (also enclosed at the end of the unit for photocopying), and give everyone a role to play.

Character Card: For | Unit 9 (Year 7)

The following characters are in favour of the new space centre and launch site:

Recommended characters:

- primary headteacher
- tourist officer
- science museum curator
- parent with young children
- politician.

Further suggestions:

grandparent

careers advisor

astronomer

businessman

engineer.

Character Card: Against | Unit 9 (Year 7)

The following characters are against the plan to build the car plant:

Recommended characters:

- representative from the Royal Society for the Protection of Birds.
- local resident with teenage children
- football coach
- member of local Ramblers' Association
- local dog walker.

Further suggestions:

headteacher of local secondary school

local road user

council representative for the Green Party

representative from the Scout Movement.

Individual Character Profiles (at the end of this unit) will offer each pupil a brief summary of his or her character's viewpoint in relation to the scenario – that is, how and why they will be affected by the outcome.

There are a total of ten characters available (five recommended characters from each side), though others may be added if necessary. All pupils in each group must receive a different role – and preferably half the roles will come from Character Card: For and the other half from Character Card Against.

Explain to the pupils what is to happen next: before the next workshop (Lesson 2), the pupils must spend time developing opinions and constructing arguments in note form, on behalf of their character. Each pupil will need to come to the group prepared to argue for or against the building of the new space centre and launch site – with good reasons to support their arguments.

Lesson 2

Begin with a circle meeting. Revisit the vision statement, core values and group pledges of the preliminary lessons. Reiterate the importance of abiding by the pledges when interacting within the group discussions that follow. Everyone must have a chance to speak and to listen.

The pupils reform the groups from Lesson 1. Give a copy of the Character Record Sheet to every pupil. Each group member will have a turn to share their opinions and arguments in respect of the proposed bill. Pupils will need to listen carefully to each other's views, noting down the names, roles and a brief two-line summary of the views of the other members in their group. Collect in the record sheets at the end of the session – and check against the original Character Profile cards.

At the end of the session, hold a short plenary in which children are invited to report back to the whole class not on their specific views and arguments, but on the process of sharing opinions – was it helpful to find others with similar views? Was there a sense of different sides forming in the group as people discovered who shared their own views and who did not? Which was easier, expressing one's own viewpoint or listening to the views of another? Did the children find themselves paying more attention to those who shared similar views to their own?

Explain to the pupils the next step in the unit – each pupil is to prepare a letter to their local MP in which they state their own views on the government's plans for the new space programme. The next workshop will be a 'public meeting' hosted by the local Member for Parliament (that is, the teacher) in which some of the letters may be read out formally, after which everyone will have the chance to speak or ask questions.

Lesson 3

The lesson begins with a short group session in which pupils who are playing the same characters across the groups get together to share ideas and thoughts, and prepare a good case. They can refer to their letters for their views if they wish. Each group of 'like-characters' will need to elect a spokesperson (someone different from the spokesperson for Unit 8). The elected speaker will address the class at the following public meeting.

Come together as a class and explain the procedure for the public meeting: there will be a table at the front of the room from which the local MP (the teacher) will chair the meeting. Sitting either side of the Chairperson will be the elected spokespersons (one of every recommended character from the character cards, that is, five on each side). The format for the meeting can be altered to suit timings and location, but a suggested order might be:

- Chairperson (the teacher) opens the meeting with an explanation of the proposed space programme that will involve the building and continued running of a space centre and launch site.

- Chairperson invites each of the characters to present their viewpoints, beginning with a supporter of the space programme and then alternating between supporters and opposers.

- Chairperson invites comments from the floor – this is an opportunity for other pupils to ask questions or express their views.

- Final vote – for this you will need to distil the different ideas into a shortlist of options. These might include:

  1. Go ahead and build the space centre and launch site.

  2. Build in collaboration with a neighbouring country, thereby sharing the cost.

  3. Do not build a space centre, but invest in another existing centre elsewhere.

  4. Do not build a space centre, or invest in space programmes elsewhere – but use the monies instead to fund other national projects and causes (for example, within health, education or the armed forces).

Once the options have been established – all pupils vote for the one they would settle for.

The different characters may well have different views – and it was very important that these were properly heard. However, once the options are listed, pupils will need to consider the question:

If I cannot have exactly what I want, what would the next best thing be?

Lesson 4

This shorter session comprises of a class discussion (out of role), in which all pupils may feedback to the rest of the group their thoughts on the role-play. The meeting can be an informal discussion loosely based around the themes of tolerance, empathy and cooperation, or you may wish to lead the session using the following questions as a guide:

- Were the group's priorities 'right' in the end? How can we tell?

- Which is more important – fixing this planet, or finding new ones?

- Can something be very good for a nation as a whole, without actually benefiting its individuals directly?

- Of what sort of things should a nation feel proud?

- Did science fiction have a part to play in influencing the way people regarded the space programme? Did people get 'carried away' with the romantic idea of travelling to new worlds?

- How exactly can you influence the morale of a nation? Would something like the space programme unite citizens?

Section 2: Follow-up Activities

Newspaper Reports

Plans to build the nation's first space centre and launch site are going ahead. As a reporter with a national newspaper, you have been given the task of breaking the news story on the front page of tomorrow's edition. Write a short piece that announces the plan; remember to include: a catchy headline, a summary of what is to be built, an artist's impression of what it may look like and comments from interested parties.

Art work

Draw an exploded diagram, or 'cross-section' of the proposed launch site. You may wish to conduct some research first of all, using the internet or library reference books, to establish what a launch site might comprise – although you can be as original as you like. Remember to include annotations (or labels) to show what and where everything is.

Debate Speech

Write a debate speech either in favour or opposing the following motion:

> *This House believes that it is time we began conserving this world properly before we go in search of new ones. Money should be spent on caring for Earthlings properly before we set about finding other life forms.*

Placards

The space centre is complete, the launch site is ready and the first manned test flight into space has been fixed for two years from now. As a member of an environmental pressure group, you decide to travel to the site and stage a peaceful protest against the funding of such an expensive 'luxury'. Design a range of mock placards that you might hold up outside the centre's perimeter fence, each one seeking to influence the people who work there to join the protest and close down the centre.

Section 3: Curriculum Overview

Curriculum Overview	National Curriculum references
Citizenship (KS3)	1g-i, 2b-c, 3a-c
English	En1: 1-11, En2: 3b, 4c-d, 5b-d; En3: 1d, 1i-k, 2a-c, 7c, 9a-d, 10.
NLS Text Types	journalistic recounts information texts, annotated designs persuasive texts: debate speech, visual texts (placards and banners).
Art and Design	1a-c, 2a, 2c, 5a-c
ICT	2a, 3a-b, 4a-c, 5a-b
Design and technology	1a-h, 3a, 7c.

Context Builder 9	Unit 9 (Year 7)

Context   A controversial space programme is planned for the country. With a space centre and launch site to rival the USA's Kennedy Space Centre and Cape Canaveral, the nation will become a major player in the race to put an astronaut on Mars... but many feel there are other more worthy needs on Earth.

Scenario   The Government has arranged a series of cluster meetings, or 'focus groups' across the country, in which members of the public are invited to share their views in response to the proposed plan to build the new space centre. One such focus group takes place in the following unit, in which very different viewpoints are revealed.

Glossary   *Controversial* – open to question; disputable or debatable.

Cluster – a gathering or group.

Worthy – deserving; admirable; worthwhile.

Character Card: For   Unit 9 (Year 7)

The following characters are in favour of the new space centre and launch site:

Recommended characters:

- primary headteacher
- tourist officer
- science museum curator
- parent with young children
- politician.

Further suggestions:

grandparent

careers advisor

astronomer

businessman

engineer.

Character Card: Against   Unit 9 (Year 7)

The following characters are against the plan to build the car plant:

Recommended characters:

- representative from the Royal Society for the Protection of Birds.
- local resident with teenage children
- football coach
- member of local Ramblers' Association
- local dog walker.

Further suggestions:

headteacher of local secondary school

local road user

council representative for the Green Party

representative from the Scout Movement.

Character Profile 1: Primary headteacher

There is nothing that excites the imagination of your pupils more than space exploration. As headteacher, you can already see the school trips being arranged to the space centre and the resulting projects in class, as the children find inspiration from watching experts at work. Maths, science, design and technology – there are so many subjects that will benefit from raising the profile of space technology for the children.

Character Profile 2: Tourist officer

The space centres and launch sites around the world not only enable countries to join the space race, they serve as huge attractions for visiting tourists, with so many people sharing a fascination with what lies beyond our atmosphere. If the nation had its own space centre, many people would have yet more reason to visit the country, and this can only be good news for the tourist industry.

Character Profile 3: Science museum curator

As curator, you know that by far the most visited resource at your museum is the space section. You feel sure that people's interest in space travel and exploration would be truly excited by the creation of a brand new space centre – and may even lead to an increased interest in science generally amongst people. Good news all round, then! You look forward to extending your space section to include some home-grown exhibits!

Character Profile 4: Parent with young children

You have often dreamed of taking your children to The Kennedy Space Centre of the famous launch site at Cape Canaveral. To have the opportunity to take them to a centre that is almost on your doorstep, well, it would be a dream come true. Developing a love of learning and an interest in science and technology is something that you feel is important in childhood, and it is never to soon to start. You look forward to inspiring your children with news of the latest launch – and who knows one day they might even be taking a space walk themselves.

Character Profile 5: Politician

The advancement of space exploration is one of the few truly great achievements for some fortunate countries; it defines a successful and prosperous economy – and it gives a country power and influence. It is the Rolls Royce parked on the drive – very expensive to ever use, but a clear symbol of prosperity. To be able to say that this country is moving forward with its own space programme, and so competing with other major players in the 'space race' is, as a politician, a dream come true. It inspires potential overseas investors to come and invest in the country's economy.

Character Profile 6: Director of a charity for homeless people

Seeking out new lands, 'boldly going' where no man has been before is all very well, but the millions and millions of pounds that such space exploration would require could provide food and shelter for a great many people back here on earth. The new space programme for the country would certainly be something to be proud of, but would it really matter to the people who still live on the streets? Wouldn't we rather be proud to boast that everyone in our country has somewhere to live? Isn't it time to fix our own land before seeking out new ones?

Character Profile 7: Medical officer

The state of the country's hospitals is not what it should be: many are desperate for more funding from the government, and some are even turning patients away due to a lack of beds or staff (or both). The government claims that there is no more money available for the health service – and now this: a multi-million pound grant to set up a space centre. As a medical officer, you fear that our priorities may be wrong. Hospitals and clinics must be at the top of the list – fanciful ideas about flying to Mars cannot be as important as saving lives and curing illnesses.

Character Profile 8: Parent with teenage children

As a parent with teenage children, you would like to see the government making education and skills a priority. More money is needed to raise standards and help school leavers gain the skills they need to get good jobs. Greater funding for university places too would help to attract students into higher education. Your children would certainly be excited to see a rocket launch – they might even be inspired – but how else would such an ambitious project impact on their lives? Exactly how many vacancies does one see for astronauts needed these days? Would it not be better to use the money to build new technical colleges and universities?

Character Profile 9: Environmental campaigner

No wonder people are keen to explore new lands – this one seems to be getting more polluted by the day. The beautiful blue and green planet seen from space is slowly getting greyer, covered in a rash of roads and cities. Is it not time we spent more time and attention on saving this planet before we give up on it and go in search of something new? The new space centre will only serve to attract more visitors, which will mean more roads, more buildings and one more patch of green gone forever. The most precious treasure in the solar system has already been found, and we are standing on it!

Character Profile 10: Military expert

You worry that in the last few years, the country's military forces have been slimmed down a great deal due to cut backs and 'reallocation' of funding. You fear that the country is now falling behind many other similar nations in terms of military might. The millions of pounds to be put aside for the proposed space centre would buy a great deal of equipment for our armed forces. As space technology advances, so too does weaponry and you believe that we must keep up with what is out there, so that we can feel safe and secure.

Character Record Sheet

Name.................................

Pupil name:	
Character role:	
Views:	

Pupil name:	
Character role:	
Views:	

Pupil name:	
Character role:	
Views:	

Pupil name:	
Character role:	
Views:	

Pupil name:	
Character role:	
Views:	

A New Chapter

Section 1: Lesson Plans

Lesson 1:

Arrange a circle meeting for the whole class. Introduce the theme for the unit by reading out the following Context Builder 10 (included at the end of this unit).

Context Builder 10	Unit 10 (Year 8)

Context	Two neighbouring senior schools, Mawdley and Cheyford High, one for boys and the other for girls respectively, are planning to combine to form a large co-educational college. Falling numbers of new entrants at Year 7 and in the lower sixth forms have forced the governors of both schools to consider merging their schools, or face closure.
Scenario	Not everyone in the schools' communities is impressed. Some feel that the existing strategy of educating boys and girls separately and then combining for social functions and events has produced fine results over many years - higher results perhaps than if they had been sharing academic classes. And what about the schools' identities? Nevertheless, as others point out, the boys and girls will be existing and working alongside each other in their future lives beyond the classroom, so why should they be segregated now?
Glossary	*Co-education* – teaching boys and girls in the same school. *Merging* – combining or absorbing into a greater whole. *Segregated* – set apart for a specific reason; dealt with separately.

Begin with a broad discussion of the purposes of education: what is it for? Is it to prepare pupils for life? Or is it for something else? Discuss how important the environment of the classroom is – and how the ethos of a school can impact on children's learning.

Elicit pupils' initial thoughts about co-educational schools and single-sex education. Identify the pupils' experience of each and discuss. Does working in a mixed class actually feel different to working in a single-sex one? How?

Establish why parents may choose to educate their sons or daughters in single-sex schools. What are the benefits? In what way might working with just boys or just girls impact on academic progress? Is it about removing the distractions? Try to establish reasons why people might oppose the merger of Mawdley and Cheyford High.

Then move to considering reasons why people in the schools' communities might support this merger. Who would support the idea of combining the boys and girls for classes? Where else in life do we find boys segregated from girls? Should it happen in schools? What might be the objections to it be? Consider the advantages of merging the two schools and establishing a co-educational college.

When everyone has had the chance to contribute, establish the groups for the unit. You may wish to record the names in each group for future lessons. Then read out the Character Cards (also enclosed at the end of this unit for photocopying) and give everyone a role to play.

Character Card: For	**Unit 10 (Year 8)**

The following characters are in favour of merging the two schools:

Recommended characters:

- parent of Year 9 pupil at Cheyford High
- registrar at Mawdley
- PSHE coordinator at Mawdley
- school Governor at Cheyford High
- head of Performing Arts at Cheyford High.

Further suggestions:

former pupil at Mawdley

careers advisor at Cheyford High

ex-parent at Mawdley (police officer)

business manager

grandparent of Cheyford High pupil.

Character Card: Against	**Unit 10 (Year 8)**

The following characters are against the merging of the two schools:

Recommended characters:

- parent of Year 9 pupil at Cheyford High
- registrar at Mawdley
- parent of Year 10 pupil at Mawdley
- director of Studies at Mawdley
- head of Pastoral Care at Cheyford High.

Further suggestions:

grandparent of Cheyford High Pupil

ex-Mawdley parent (and retired examiner)

grandparent of Mawdley pupil

former pupil at Cheyford High

local university lecturer.

Individual Character Profiles will offer each pupil a brief summary of his or her character's viewpoint in relation to the scenario – that is, how and why they will be affected by the outcome.

There are a total of ten characters available (five from each side), though others may be added if necessary.

Explain to the pupils what is to happen next: before the next workshop (Lesson 2), the pupils must spend time developing opinions and constructing arguments in note form, on behalf of their character. Each pupil will need to come to the group prepared to argue for or against merger of Mawdley and Cheyford High – with good reasons to support their arguments. Speakers will do well to consider the interests of the whole community – showing how the merger will benefit or disadvantage many people (rather than just themselves).

Lesson 2

Begin with a circle meeting. Revisit the vision statement, core values and group pledges of the preliminary lessons. Reiterate the importance of abiding by the pledges when interacting within the group discussions that follow. Everyone must have a chance to speak and to listen.

The pupils reform the groups from Lesson 1. Give a copy of the Character Record Sheet to every pupil. Each group member will have a turn to share their opinions and arguments in respect of the proposed merger. Pupils will need to listen carefully to each other, noting down the names, roles and a brief two-line summary of the views of the other members in their group. Collect in the record sheets at the end of the session – and check against the original Character Profile cards.

At the end of the session, hold a short plenary in which children are invited to report back to the whole class not on their specific views and arguments, but on the process of sharing opinions – was it helpful to find others with similar views? Was there a sense of different sides forming in the group as people discovered who shared their own views and who did not? Which was easier, expressing one's own viewpoint or listening to the views of another? Did the children find themselves paying more attention to those who shared similar views to their own?

Explain to the pupils the next step in the unit – each pupil is to prepare a letter to the leader of the Local Education Authority in which they state their own views on the plan to merge Mawdley and Cheyford High. The next workshop will be a 'public meeting' hosted by the education authority's leader (that is, the teacher) in which some of the letters may be read out formally, after which everyone will have the chance to speak or ask questions.

Lesson 3

The lesson begins with a short group session in which pupils who are playing the same characters across the groups get together to share ideas and thoughts, and prepare a good case. They can refer to their letters for their views if they wish. Each group of 'like-characters' will need to elect a spokesperson (some one different from the spokesperson for Unit 9). The elected speaker will address the class at the following public meeting.

Come together as a class and explain the procedure for the public meeting: there will be a table at the front of the room from which the leader of the education authority (the teacher) will chair the meeting. Sitting either side of the chairperson will be the elected spokespersons (one of every recommended character from the character cards, that is, five on each side). The format for the meeting can be altered to suit timings and location, but a suggested order might be:

- Chairperson (the teacher) opens the meeting with an explanation of the current problem of falling numbers at the two schools, and of the plan to merge the two.

- Chairperson invites each of the characters to present their viewpoints, beginning with a supporter of the merger and then alternating between supporters and opposers.

132

- Chairperson invites comments from the floor – this is an opportunity for other pupils to ask questions or express their views.

- Final vote – for this you will need to distil the different ideas into a shortlist of options. These might include:

  1. Go ahead with the plan to merge the schools.

  2. Merge the schools, but keep academic classes as single-sex environments – with boys and girls coming together for daily registration, PSHE lessons and various creative projects.

  3. Do not merge the schools, but share resources and facilities, running the two schools as separate concerns, but funded and governed by the same body.

  4. Keep the status quo and find new ways to recruit and retain more pupils, setting up an appeal for funds.

The different characters may well have different views – and it was very important that these were properly heard. However, once the options are listed, pupils will need to consider the question:

If I cannot have exactly what I want, what would the next best thing be?

It may be useful here to revisit the vision and core values of the preliminary lessons, to remind the pupils of the core objectives and the need for consensus.

Lesson 4

This shorter session comprises of a class discussion (out of role), in which all pupils may feedback to the rest of the group their thoughts on the role-play. The meeting can be an informal discussion loosely based around the themes of tolerance, empathy and cooperation, or you may wish to lead the session using the following questions as a guide:

- Which was more important in the schools: achieving high grades or developing good interpersonal skills and learning to mix well?

- Were people able to see both sides? Was their empathy in the group?

- Do you think some people might find it difficult looking beyond the needs and welfare of their own children?

- Have you altered your view of the purpose of education now?

- If the merger went ahead, how would you support the disgruntled parents and staff who had opposed it?

Section 2: Follow-up Activities

Debate Speech

Hold a class debate in which pupils deliver speeches proposing or opposing the following motion:

This House believes that boys and girls should be taught separately for all academic subjects. Co-education does not adequately serve the disparate needs of pupils.

History Topic

Research the origins of single-sex education and co-education. When were boys and girls first segregated and why? Find examples of schools that first pioneered the idea. To what extent were the children separated – for academic lessons only, or in the playground too? In some Victorian schools for example, girls played in one half of the playground and boys in another! Consider any opposition to these plans – when (and why) did people demand something different?

Diaries

Imagine you are one of the pupils at Mawdley or Cheyford High. Write a diary entry that describes how you feel on the first day of term at the newly merged co-educational college. What has changed for you? Do you feel nervous or excited? Describe how the dynamics of your class might feel different now. What exactly has changed for you?

Letters

Imagine you are the headteacher of Mawdley or Cheyford High. The merger has now been approved and will go ahead later this year. Your task is to write to all parents, explaining the decision and drumming up support for the merger. Remember to consider the viewpoints of all parents, some of which will be disgruntled to say the least! Your letter will need to be informative, but persuasive too, sharing the news of the merger in as positive a way as possible.

Section 3: Curriculum Overview

Curriculum Overview	National Curriculum references
Citizenship (KS3)	1g, 2a-c, 3a-c
PSHE	1b, 2c, 3a-e, 3i, 3k
English	En1: 1a-g, 2b-f, 3a-b, 4a, 8a-c, 9c, 10a-b; En2: 1d, 2h, 4c, 9a-b; En3: 1d, 1e-g, 1l-n, 9b-c
NLS Text Types	jpersonal recounts (diaries) chronological reports (history topics) persuasive texts: formal letters and speeches. Context Builder 10.

Context Builder 10	Unit 10 (Year 8)

Context
Two neighbouring senior schools, Mawdley and Cheyford High, one for boys and the other for girls respectively, are planning to combine to form a large co-educational college. Falling numbers of new entrants at Year 7 and in the lower sixth forms have forced the governors of both schools to consider merging their schools, or face closure.

Scenario
Not everyone in the schools' communities is impressed. Some feel that the existing strategy of educating boys and girls separately and then combining for social functions and events has produced fine results over many years - higher results perhaps than if they had been sharing academic classes. And what about the schools' identities? Nevertheless, as others point out, the boys and girls will be existing and working alongside each other in their future lives beyond the classroom, so why should they be segregated now?

Glossary
Co-education – teaching boys and girls in the same school.

Merging – combining or absorbing into a greater whole.

Segregated – set apart for a specific reason; dealt with separately.

Character Card (For)   Unit 10 (Year 8)

The following characters are in favour of merging the two schools:

Recommended characters:

- parent of Year 9 pupil at Cheyford High
- registrar at Mawdley
- PSHE coordinator at Mawdley
- school Governor at Cheyford High
- head of Performing Arts at Cheyford High.

Further suggestions:

former pupil at Mawdley

careers advisor at Cheyford High

ex-parent at Mawdley (police officer)

business manager

grandparent of Cheyford High pupil.

Character Card: Against   Unit 10 (Year 8)

The following characters are against the merging of the two schools:

Recommended characters:

- parent of Year 9 pupil at Cheyford High
- registrar at Mawdley
- parent of Year 10 pupil at Mawdley
- director of Studies at Mawdley
- head of Pastoral Care at Cheyford High.

Further suggestions:

grandparent of Cheyford High Pupil

ex-Mawdley parent (and retired examiner)

grandparent of Mawdley pupil

former pupil at Cheyford High

local university lecturer.

Character Profile 1: Parent of Year 9 pupil at Cheyford High

As a parent with a daughter in Year 9 at Cheyford High, you are anxious to make sure that you give her the best possible preparation for her future life beyond the classroom. You had mixed feelings about sending her to an all-girls' school initially, but the only other co-educational school in the area was some distance away. Though the teaching has been good so far, and her grades impressive, you feel she would benefit from the social interaction of a mixed school, bringing her the confidence she will need to compete for jobs in the future and to form positive relationships with friends and colleagues.

Character Profile 2: Registrar at Mawdley

You have been concerned about the falling numbers of pupils registering for Mawdley in recent months. The last few years in fact show an unsettling decrease in applications which, if it continues, will mean the school may even face closure. Merging with your neighbour in this way may change the identity of Mawdley, but it could be the beginning of a new and exciting chapter, both in your career and in the life of the two schools.

Character Profile 3: PSHE coordinator at Mawdley

The academic results at Mawdley are high and the school enjoys a fine reputation for sport, but as the member of staff responsible for PSHE, your concern is for the social development of the pupils – and you suspect that, for some boys at least, being in an environment without girls is having a detrimental effect on their behaviour. You feel that the proposed merger of the two schools would certainly give the children a more rounded social education. Your aim is to help the children to become active citizens in the world – and it is a world of men and women!

Character Profile 4: School governor at Cheyford High

You are not sure that the debate about whether to go to co-education is relevant here; it is more about whether to stay open and survive, or face closure. Joining forces with neighbouring Mawdley will ensure that both schools have a future – and an exciting one at that. New buildings, a new curriculum, a new ethos about the place – all good news for a school that is on the brink of being closed down by the local education authority. Better for the girls to be studying alongside boys than not at all.

Character Profile 5: Head of Performing Arts at Cheyford High

Though the productions at Cheyford High have enjoyed a good reputation over the years, as the new Head of Performing Arts, you would relish the opportunity to combine with Mawdley – a merger that would not only see some exciting new drama and dance studios being built, but also would pave the way for so many more productions now that the cast is a mixed one! You can already picture your opening night of West Side Story!

Character Profile 6: Head of Games at Mawdley

Unless the new co-educational college has equal numbers of netball courts, hockey pitches and rugby pitches, (which is unlikely), which sport is going to take precedence when the merger has happened? You are worried that Mawdley's outstanding reputation for sporting achievements will be affected – not from any lack of skill from the girls, who enjoy a similar reputation – but from a lack of facilities that cater for the vast range of sports that you will need to offer when the boys and girls combine. There simply just won't be the money, some sports may have to take a back seat.

Character Profile 7: Catering Manager at Cheyford High

If or when the new merger takes place, and Mawdley combines with Cheyford to become a central college, will you and your team of chefs still have jobs? Will there be two kitchens? There may be double the number of students, and so clearly more staff will be needed, but with only one large kitchen to share – will it be a case of too many cooks spoiling the broth? And who will be in charge anyway?

Character Profile 8: Parent of Year 10 pupil at Mawdley

You know your son very well – and you know that if he had the opportunity to study alongside girls in class, his attention would not necessarily be devoted to his schoolwork entirely! You have been pleased with way his grades have progressed since putting your son at Mawdley; compared to his progress at a previous, co-educational school, he has done very well indeed. You fear that if the merger goes ahead, it may be back to his old ways of caring more about the class gossip than about his work. Preparing them to build relationships is a good thing – but school is about passing exams too isn't it?

Character Profile 9: Director of Studies at Mawdley

As the person with responsibility for delivering the academic curriculum at Mawdley, and monitoring the boys' progress, you are concerned that the merger could well have a negative impact on their work. You are not convinced that the boys' academic progress will continue at the same rate if they join the girls in co-educational classes. Statistics often show that in a Key Stage 3 class of girls and boys, the girls achieve better grades than the boys overall, but here at Mawdley, you are proud that the grades are as high as your neighbours' at Cheyford. Will it last?

Character Profile 10: Head of Pastoral Care at Cheyford High

As head of Pastoral Care, your role has much to do with the girls' general wellbeing: their health and happiness at school. Cheyford High is a safe and very happy place with a positive and productive ethos. You are proud of the support offered to the pupils, particularly when they encounter problems. You are pleased that most girls find it easy to talk to staff and share their worries. Though you know the same good work happens at Mawdley, you fear that when sharing the same class, some girls and boys may soon become withdrawn and less willing to show they have a problem.

Character Record Sheet

Name..................................

Pupil name:
Character role:
Views:

Pupil name:
Character role:
Views:

Pupil name:
Character role:
Views:

Pupil name:
Character role:
Views:

Pupil name:
Character role:
Views:

High Tides

Section 1: Lesson Plans

Lesson 1

Arrange a circle meeting for the whole class. Introduce the theme for the unit by reading out the following Context Builder 11 (enclosed at the end of this unit).

Context Builder 11	Unit 11 (Year 8)
Context	*High Tides* is a new television series to be set in the fictional town of Springs Cove. The actual location proposed for the filming is the quaint fishing port of Fencombe, where opinion is much divided over whether they should let the film crews into their otherwise tranquil coastal community.
Scenario	After receiving so many letters from concerned residents, Fencombe borough council has called a public meeting in which views can be shared and a decision can be reached over whether the new series should be set in Fencombe at all.
Glossary	*Quaint* – attractively old-fashioned; having historic charm. *Tranquil* – peaceful; without noisy distraction.

Begin with a brief discussion of how fictional soap operas are set in real life towns – how we may take for granted that real communities are affected by fictional storylines and filming schedules.

Explore further how television programmes may affect daily life for residents living in a film location. What experience of watching soap operas have the children had? Which locations do they think are real and which might be film studios? Invite the children to share their thoughts. Has anyone visited a 'real town' that is the setting for a fictional drama? What was it like? Did it live up to expectations, or was it different in some ways?

Elicit pupils' thoughts about the advantages there might be in playing host to a film crew. Consider the knock-on effects on tourism and local business. Why would residents wish to put their particular town 'on the map'?

When everyone has had the chance to contribute, establish the groups for the unit. You may wish to record the names in each group for future lessons. Then read out the following Character Cards (photocopiable versions appear at the end of the unit) and give everyone a role to play.

Character Card (For) Unit 11 (Year 8)

The following characters support the plan to bring *High Tides* to Fencombe:

Recommended characters:

- tourist information centre manager
- hotel owner
- parent with teenage children
- local estate agent
- local fisherman.

Further suggestions:

headteacher of Fencombe County Primary

elderly resident

community welfare officer

youth leader

restaurant manager.

Character Card: Against Unit 11 (Year 8)

The following characters oppose the plan to film *High Tides* in Fencombe:

Recommended characters:

- local resident
- local fisherman
- parent with young children
- police officer
- elderly resident.

Further suggestions:

bank manager

harbour master

regular holidaymaker (visits Fencombe every year)

traffic warden

clerical worker in Fencombe.

Individual Character Profiles will offer each pupil a brief summary of his or her character's viewpoint in relation to the scenario – that is, how and why they will be affected by the outcome.

There are a total of ten characters available (five recommended characters from each side), though others may be added if necessary. All pupils in each group must receive a different role – and preferably half the roles will come from Character Card: For and the other half from Character Card Against.

Explain to the pupils what is to happen next: before the next workshop (Lesson 2), the pupils must spend time developing opinions and constructing arguments in note form, on behalf of their character. Each pupil will need to come to the group prepared to argue for or against the plan to film *High Tides* in Fencombe – with good reasons to support their arguments. Speakers will do well to consider the interests of the whole community – showing how filming project may benefit or disadvantage many people (rather than just themselves).

Lesson 2

Begin with a circle meeting. Revisit the vision statement, core values and group pledges of the preliminary lessons. Reiterate the importance of abiding by the pledges when interacting within the group discussions that follow. Everyone must have a chance to speak and to listen.

The pupils reform the groups from Lesson 1. Give a copy of the Character Record Sheet to every pupil. Each group member will have a turn to share their opinions and arguments in respect of the proposed plan to film the television series in Fencombe. Pupils will need to listen carefully to each other, noting down the names, roles and a brief two-line summary of the views of the other members in their group. Collect in the record sheets at the end of the session – and check against the original Character Profile cards.

At the end of the session, hold a short plenary in which children are invited to report back to the whole class not on their specific views and arguments, but on the process of sharing opinions – was it helpful to find others with similar views? Was there a sense of different sides forming in the group as people discovered who shared their own views and who did not? Which was easier, expressing one's own viewpoint or listening to the views of another? Did the children find themselves paying more attention to those who shared similar views to their own?

Explain to the pupils the next step in the unit – each pupil is to prepare a letter to the town council in which they state their own views on the plan to use Fencombe as the setting for *High Tides*. The next workshop will be a 'public meeting' hosted by the leader of Fencombe council (that is, the teacher) in which some of the letters may be read out formally, after which everyone will have the chance to speak or ask questions.

Lesson 3

The lesson begins with a short group session in which pupils who are playing the same characters across the groups get together to share ideas and thoughts, and prepare a good case. They can refer to their letters for their views if they wish. Each group of 'like-characters' will need to elect a spokesperson (some one different from the spokesperson for Unit 10). The elected speaker will address the class at the following public meeting.

Come together as a class and explain the procedure for the public meeting: there will be a table at the front of the room from which the leader of the local council (the teacher) will chair the meeting. Sitting either side of the chairperson will be the elected spokespersons (one of every recommended character from the character cards, that is, five on each side). The format for the meeting can be altered to suit timings and location, but a suggested order might be:

- Chairperson (that is, the teacher) opens the meeting with an explanation of the proposed plan to use Fencombe as the location for the fictional drama *High Tides*.

- Chairperson invites each of the characters to present their view points, beginning with a supporter of the plan and then alternating between supporters and opposers.

- Chairperson invites comments from the floor – this is an opportunity for other pupils to ask questions or express their views.

- Final vote – for this you will need to distil the different ideas into a shortlist of options. These might include:

  1. Continue with the plan to use Fencombe as the location for *High Tides*.

  2. Choose a different coastal resort as the main host town (to be Spring Cove), but allow the film company to shoot some scenes in Fencombe.

  3. Do not allow any filming in Fencombe.

The different characters may well have different views – and it was very important that these were properly heard. However, once the options are listed, pupils will need to consider the question:

If I cannot have exactly what I want, what would the next best thing be?

It may be useful here to revisit the vision and core values of the preliminary lessons, to remind the pupils of the core objectives and the need for a consensus.

Lesson 4

This shorter session comprises of a class discussion (out of role), in which all pupils may feedback to the rest of the group their thoughts on the role-play. The meeting can be an informal discussion loosely based around the themes of tolerance, empathy and cooperation, or you may wish to lead the session using the following questions as a guide:

- Did we find that good news for someone can be bad news for another?

- Is television too powerful? Have we allowed it to take over our lives too much?

- Should we allow cameras in to people's real daily lives in this way? Should we respect a whole town's privacy?

- Would the townsfolk of a real town in similar circumstances actually get to have they say on such matters? Whose decision would it be to let the camera in?

- How might one reach a compromise in real life?

Section 2: Follow-up Activities

Diary

Write a diary entry for a young resident of Fencombe, describing the first day that the cameras appeared in town. What was it like? Did it seem strange seeing actors pretending to be the residents of your own town? Did you feel territorial? Did you welcome your guests? Try to record not only what happened, but also your reactions in response to the events of the day as they unfold. Perhaps your expectations were exceeded.

Script

Explore possible opening scenes for the very first episode of *High Tides*. What might the opening storyline be? Write a few pages of script for the first few minutes of episode one. Consider the stage directions – location, camera angles, weather, sound effects and so on.

Trailer

You have been given the task of marketing the soap opera, *High Tides*. Write a series of possible one-minute trailers for the new series. What might you include in the opening shots? How might you grab viewers' attention and inspire them to catch the first episode when it is aired? Consider how the advertisement might be adapted for the radio.

History / Geography – Settlement Study

Choose a small-sized fishing community and research its origins. How dependent has the town been on fishing – years ago and nowadays? Are there other forms of industry that have superseded fishing in the locality? To what extent does the fishing port resemble its original landscape? Are there any new industries that have attracted migrants to the town? Are there any push or pull factors that might have influenced movement of residents in the area? To what extend are its population governed by the natural landscape?

Section 3: Curriculum Overview

Curriculum Overview	National Curriculum references
Citizenship	1g, 1h, 2a-c, 3a-c
PSHE	1b, 2c, 3a-e, 3i, 3k, 4f, 4g
Geography	1a, 3c-d, 4a-b, 5b, 6g,
English	En1: 1a-g, 2b-f, 3a-b, 4a, 8a-c, 9c, 10b, 11a En2: 1d, 2h, 4c, 9a-b; En3: 1d, 1e-g, 1l-n, 9b-c
NLS Text Types	personal recounts (diaries) playscripts non-chronological reports (history / geography settlement study) persuasive texts: fictional advertisements.

Context Builder 11	Unit 11 (Year 8)

Context   *High Tides* is a new television series to be set in the fictional town of Springs Cove. The actual location proposed for the filming is the quaint fishing port of Fencombe, where opinion is much divided over whether they should let the film crews into their otherwise tranquil coastal community.

Scenario   After receiving so many letters from concerned residents, Fencombe borough council has called a public meeting in which views can be shared and a decision can be reached over whether the new series should be set in Fencombe at all.

Glossary   *Quaint* – attractively old-fashioned; having historic charm.

Tranquil – peaceful; without noisy distraction.

Character Card: For

The following characters support the plan to bring *High Tides* to Fencombe:

Recommended characters:

- tourist information centre manager
- hotel owner
- parent with teenage children
- local estate agent
- local fisherman.

Further suggestions:

headteacher of Fencombe County Primary

elderly resident

community welfare officer

youth leader

restaurant manager.

Character Card: Against

The following characters oppose the plan to film *High Tides* in Fencombe:

Recommended characters:

- local resident
- local fisherman
- parent with young children
- police officer
- elderly resident.

Further suggestions:

bank manager

harbour master

regular holidaymaker (visits Fencombe every year)

traffic warden

clerical worker in Fencombe.

Character Profile 1: Tourist Information Centre Manager

When film crews have used other locations as the fictional settings of television series, the interest in the real towns has been high, with many more tourists visiting the area, all bringing business to the local community. Fencombe may be no exception; once viewers discover that they can actually visit 'Spring Cove' and see for themselves the buildings and harbour that usually appear on screen, the town will become a thriving tourist attraction, rather than the sleepy place it is now.

Character Profile 2: Hotel owner

Business in this quiet little port may thrive during the summer months, but what of the other three quarters of the year? As a hotelier you never really know whether you will make it through the long and quiet winters to the next holiday season. Creating a fictional series set in Fencombe will really put the place on the map all year round – and, with luck, will bring more guests both for you and for many of your friends who also rely upon tourists for their livelihood.

Character Profile 3: Parent with teenage children

Your children are growing up fast and wanting new distractions everyday. Living in such a pretty fishing port may seem idyllic to some, but for young teenagers, there is precious little to do. It is when your children are bored that they may just find mischief! What better a distraction then than to be able to watch film crews in action on their doorstep – and who knows, they may even get parts as extras. If *High Tides* gives your children something to amuse them and perhaps even inspire them, then it cannot be a bad idea.

Character Profile 4: Local estate agent

Property prices are already fairly strong in this pretty fishing village, but there is always room for inflation! You would love to be able to say in the property particulars that potential purchasers would be buying their own piece of 'Spring Cove' – imagine the premiums you could put on the properties then! You are sure that business would pick up even further if the film crew were allowed to put Fencombe on the map once and for all.
The television series would be a super advertisement for your patch of coastline!

Character Profile 5: Local fisherman

Business has been slow of late, with fish stocks running low. Like so many fishermen, you have had to begin supplementing your income by offering short sailing trips to visitors. If the television series comes to Fencombe, so too will more tourists in time, and this should mean a great many more fee-paying passengers on your boat. From out in the bay you will be able to show them great views of Spring Cove (perhaps as it appears in the television credits at the beginning of each episode!).

Character Profile 6: Local resident

One of the reasons why you moved to Fencombe was to enjoy a quiet, undisturbed existence on a particularly unspoilt stretch of coastline. Fencombe's main appeal for you is the fact that few people in the country have heard of it, or know of its beauty – and that's how you'd like it to stay! Bringing in television cameras is just about the worst idea you have heard since moving to this pretty place years ago. One thing is for sure, if *High Tides* comes to town, things in Fencombe will never be the same again.

Character Profile 7: Local fisherman

You have never enjoyed being an exhibit for the tourists. Each summer it is always the same: peer over your shoulder and you see a dozen new visitors, all merrily snapping away with their cameras at one of the last remaining authentic fishermen on this stretch of coastline. You are
not a fictional character from a new soap opera, fishing is your livelihood and, though business is hard at the present, you have never succumbed to ferrying tourists around like some of your friends have. Fencombe is a quiet, working fishing port – one of the last remaining. You don't have the time to be clambering over television crews and inquisitive fans of the show!

Character Profile 8: Parent with young children

Trying to navigate the tiny, busy streets and crowded cobbled pavements is never easy, but with a baby in a pushchair and a toddler on reigns, it is virtually impossible. When the 'silly' season comes and the tourists arrive in town you often feel frustrated if you cannot find anywhere to park! The idea of lorry loads of television cameras all blocking the traffic and taking over shops for that 'ideal shot' sounds pretty horrendous to a local like you with errands to run!

Character Profile 9: Police officer

You worry that the film crews that may come to Fencombe would cause just too much disruption for the locals to bear – and this could well end in the odd incident of road rage. As a local law enforcement officer, you like to have contented residents – they keep out of trouble, usually. When the town becomes congested, and people become frustrated, the peaceful town of Fencombe becomes as fraught as anywhere else in the country! To keep traffic moving freely, and the streets uncluttered, it may well be that *High Tides* might have to find another Spring Cove!

Character Profile 10: Elderly resident

You like watching television, and often enjoy a good soap opera, but bringing this new show to Fencombe spells bad news. You have lived in this peaceful setting for over seventy years – and it has remained largely unspoiled in that time. It may be the ideal place for *High Tides* – and viewers would certainly enjoy seeing shots of this lovely fishing port – but this will be of no comfort when you wish to get to the post office and find you can't because the road has been shut for filming – again!

Character Record Sheet

Name...................................

Pupil name:
Character role:
Views:

Pupil name:
Character role:
Views:

Pupil name:
Character role:
Views:

Pupil name:
Character role:
Views:

Pupil name:
Character role:
Views:

A Modern Revolution

Section 1: Lesson Plans

Lesson 1

Arrange a circle meeting for the whole class. Introduce the theme for the unit by reading out the following Context Builder 12 (enclosed at the end of this unit).

Context Builder 12	**Unit 12 (Year 8)**
Context	After years of debate, the Government is now close to passing the Republic Act, a bill that will see the monarchy consigned to the history books as the people elect a president as their ceremonial figurehead. The Prime Minister and the Government are to remain in power.
Scenario	The Government have arranged for a series of focus groups to take place across the country, in which a range of people from different walks of life come together to share their views on the Republic Act. In this scenario one such focus group comes together to debate the bill.
Glossary	*Republic* – a state in which supreme power is held by the people and their elected representatives (with an elected or nominated President rather than a hereditary monarchy).
	Ceremonial – a role or duty involving only nominal authority or power.

Begin with a brief discussion of the role of the monarchy through the ages – how has it changed?

Consider how powerful the monarch would have been in years gone by – then consider what actual powers the monarchy has now. Think about the difference between a president and a monarch. Ensure pupils understand that one is elected and the other is a hereditary, ceremonial title.

Consider reasons why people should want to do away with the monarchy – to elect a president instead. Mention ideas of democracy, justice, fairness. What about the church? Years ago many people believed that the monarch was 'God's own representative on Earth.' How do people feel about that now? What exactly is a monarch's role? How can he or she affect the lives of citizens (or subjects)? Why might a president be better?

Then move on to thinking about the benefits of being a country with its own royal family. Consider notions of continuity, strength, power and so on. Think about the reputation that the royal family may have abroad. How is our country regarded by others? Is our royal family an integral part of how we are perceived? Why might others be envious of our having a monarchy? Consider the good that the royal family do abroad – for charity, for business and political relations.

When everyone has had the chance to contribute, establish the groups for the unit. You may wish to record the names in each group for future lessons. Then read out the following Character Cards (also enclosed at the end of the unit, for photocopying), and give everyone a role to play.

Character Card: For

The following characters support the Republic Act:

Recommended characters:

- hospital worker
- director of a charity for homeless people
- parent with young children
- university student
- tax payer on a low income.

Further suggestions:

headteacher of a large primary school

member of the European Parliament (MEP)

lawyer

youth leader

university lecturer (teaching politics).

Character Card: Against

The following characters oppose the Republic Act:

Recommended characters:

- tourist officer
- retired army Major
- headteacher of a comprehensive school
- business manager (travels extensively overseas)
- journalist.

Further suggestions:

historian

retired taxi driver

hotel manager

shop keeper

lawyer.

Individual Character Profiles (at the end of this unit) will offer each pupil a brief summary of his or her character's viewpoint in relation to the scenario – that is, how and why they will be affected by the outcome.

There are a total of ten characters available (five recommended characters from each side), though others may be added if necessary. All pupils in each group must receive a different role – and preferably half the roles will come from Character Card: For and the other half from Character Card Against.

Explain to the pupils what is to happen next: before the next workshop (Lesson 2), the pupils must spend time developing opinions and constructing arguments in note form, on behalf of their character. Each pupil will need to come to the group prepared to argue for or against the Republic Act – with good reasons to support their arguments. Speakers will do well to consider the interests of the whole community – showing how losing a monarchy may affect the country as a whole (rather than just themselves).

Lesson 2

Begin with a circle meeting. Revisit the vision statement, core values and group pledges of the preliminary lessons. Reiterate the importance of abiding by the pledges when interacting within the group discussions that follow. Everyone must have a chance to speak and to listen.

The pupils reform the groups from Lesson 1. Give a copy of the Character Record Sheet to every pupil. Each group member will have a turn to share their opinions and arguments in respect of the plan to abolish the monarchy. Pupils will need to listen carefully to each other, noting down the names, roles and a brief two-line summary of the views of the other members in their group. Collect in the record sheets at the end of the session – and check against the original Character Profile cards.

At the end of the session, hold a short plenary in which children are invited to report back to the whole class not on their specific views and arguments, but on the process of sharing opinions – was it helpful to find others with similar views? Was there a sense of different sides forming in the group as people discovered who shared their own views and who did not? Which was easier, expressing one's own viewpoint or listening to the views of another? Did the children find themselves paying more attention to those who shared similar views to their own?

Explain to the pupils the next step in the unit – each pupil is to prepare a letter to their local MP in which they state their own views on the plan to bring in the Republic Act. The next workshop will be a 'focus feedback' meeting hosted by the local MP (the teacher) in which some of the letters may be read out formally, after which everyone will have the chance to speak or ask questions.

Lesson 3

The lesson begins with a short group session in which pupils who are playing the same characters across the groups get together to share ideas and thoughts, and prepare a good case. They can refer to their letters for their views if they wish. Each group of 'like-characters' will need to elect a spokesperson (some one different from the spokesperson for Unit 11). The elected speaker will address the class at the following focus feedback meeting.

Come together as a class and explain the procedure for the meeting: there will be a table at the front of the room from which the local Member of Parliament (the teacher) will chair the meeting. Sitting either side of the chairperson will be the elected spokespersons (one of every recommended character from the character cards: that is, five on each side). The format for the meeting can be altered to suit timings and location, but a suggested order might be:

- Chairperson (the teacher) opens the meeting with an explanation of the proposed Republic Act, its powers and consequences.

- Chairperson invites each of the characters to present their viewpoints, beginning with a supporter of the bill and then alternating between supporters and opposers.

- Chairperson invites comments from the floor – this is an opportunity for other pupils to ask questions or express their views.

- Final vote – for this you will need to distil the different ideas into a shortlist of options. These might include:

  1. Approve the bill – which will then be passed by Parliament and become the Republic Act, abolishing the monarchy in favour of an elected President.

  2. Recommend alterations to the bill before it can be passed – for example, inserting a clause that allows for the monarchy to be returned, should the new republic fail.

  3. Abandon plans for the bill and retain the status quo (that is, the monarchy remains).

The different characters may well have different views – and it was very important that these were properly heard. However, once the options are listed, pupils will need to consider the question:

If I cannot have exactly what I want, what would the next best thing be?

It may be useful here to revisit the vision and core values of the preliminary lessons, to remind the pupils of the core objectives and the need for a consensus.

Lesson 4

This shorter session comprises of a class discussion (out of role), in which all pupils may feedback to the rest of the group their thoughts on the role-play. The meeting can be an informal discussion loosely based around the themes of tolerance, empathy and cooperation, or you may wish to lead the session using the following questions as a guide:

- Did people's beliefs run deep? Why might that be?

- Is the idea of a monarchy embedded in our psyche somehow, such as the church or school?

- Was it difficult trying to separate one's own views from the needs of the country as a whole?

- Can something be bad for individual citizens but very good for the nation as a whole?

- What were the stumbling blocks to reaching consensus? The notion of privilege? Trying to make things more 'fair'?

- What does the term 'royalist' mean? What might its antonym be?

- Do you think such a debate might ever be aired in public in real life?

Section 2: Follow-up Activities

Dialogue

Write the dialogue for a short conversation between two drinkers in a pub, discussing their views on whether to abolish the monarchy or not. One person holds strong royalist views, while the other believes it is time to elect a president instead. Try to include interesting synonyms for 'said' each time, and add adverbs for effect too, for example, 'he retorted sarcastically.'

Debate Speech

Write a debate speech proposing or opposing the following motion:

This House believes that the monarchy is out of favour and out of date with the modern world. It is time to build a Republic fit for the twenty-first century.

Geography Project

Conduct research to find out how many royal dynasties there are in Europe. Which countries have a monarch and which have an elected president? In what ways do you think the countries differ as a result of having a royal family or a president? What is lost and what is gained?

History Projects

Choose a monarch from history and assess the extent of their powers, compared with today's royal family. To what degree did the king or queen 'rule' the country back then? Would anyone have dared to suggest abolishing the monarchy then? What would have happened if they had? Focus particularly on the idea that many people believed the monarch was 'God's own representative on Earth. How did this affect the monarch's reign?

Consider a time when such a revolution actually happened in a country. What were the effects, both short term and long term? How have the political and cultural landscapes of the country altered as a consequence?

Journalistic Report

Imagine that the Republic Act has been passed and the monarchy is to be replaced by an elected president. Can you imagine the impact that this would have on the nation when the announcement that the bill has been approved is finally made? Plan out how a newspaper might run this momentous story – consider the best headline, the most suitable photographs and the opening paragraphs.

Section 3: Curriculum Overview

Curriculum Overview	National Curriculum references
Citizenship	1g, 1h, 2a-c, 3a-c
PSHE	1b, 2c, 3a-e, 3i, 3k, 4f, 4g
Geography	1a, 3c-d, 4a-b, 6i
History	2c, 3a, 7b, 8, 11
English	En1: 1a-g, 2b-f, 3a-b, 4a, 8a-c, 9c, 10a, 11a En2: 1c, 2h, 3a, 4c, 5d, 9a-b; En3: 1d, 1e-g, 1i-k, 9b-d
NLS Text Types	playscripts / dialogue in prose persuasive text: debate speeches non-chronological reports (history / geography research) discursive texts: essays on views of the monarchy.

Context Builder 12   **Unit 12 (Year 8)**

Context   After years of debate, the Government is now close to passing the Republic Act, a bill that will see the monarchy consigned to the history books as the people elect a president as their ceremonial figurehead. The Prime Minister and the Government are to remain in power.

Scenario   The Government have arranged for a series of focus groups to take place across the country, in which a range of people from different walks of life come together to share their views on the Republic Act. In this scenario one such focus group comes together to debate the bill.

Glossary   *Republic* – a state in which supreme power is held by the people and their elected representatives (with an elected or nominated President rather than a hereditary monarchy).

Ceremonial – a role or duty involving only nominal authority or power.

Character Card: For

The following characters support the Republic Act:

Recommended characters:

- hospital worker
- director of a charity for homeless people
- parent with young children
- university student
- tax payer on a low income.

Further suggestions:

headteacher of a large primary school

member of the European Parliament (MEP)

lawyer

youth leader

university lecturer (teaching politics).

Character Card: Against

The following characters oppose the Republic Act:

Recommended characters:

- tourist officer
- retired army Major
- headteacher of a comprehensive school
- business manager (travels extensively overseas)
- journalist.

Further suggestions:

historian

retired taxi driver

hotel manager

shop keeper

lawyer.

Character Profile 1: Hospital worker

Rolling out the red carpet and indulging in royal handshakes is all very well, but how exactly does that help you or you patients in the poorly-funded hospital in which you earn a pittance? The royal family have royal surgeons to care for them. They have hospital wings reserved for them, while you are forced to squeeze patients into rooms together, with others lying in beds in corridors, waiting for treatment. It all seems so unfair. Having an elected President may not make a huge difference to your life, but it might seem a little more just.

Character Profile 2: Director of a charity for homeless people

There are many homeless people living on the streets of the capital, a short walk from the one of the largest, most luxurious residencies in the world – the royal family's home. Its residents have not been elected – they have inherited their wealth and their positions as head of state. You feel sure that some of the crown's great fortune could so easily be used to wipe out homelessness for good. Yet when the tourists come to see the palace, the homeless people on the streets are told to move on; they are unsightly.

Character Profile 3: Parent with young children

You wonder how you will explain to your children as they grow in the twenty-first century exactly why a select few people are regarded as the most important family in the country simply because of their bloodline. The country is a proud nation of brave men and women who have achieved great things – from great heroes of industry to the courageous soldiers of great wars, paying the ultimate price so their countrymen can be free. Your children will grow to be proud of their fellow compatriots, for what they have achieved rather than who they are or what position they have inherited.

Character Profile 4: University student

As a student of European Studies, you believe that modern republics are the most successful, democratic nations. Their people work together for the good of their country, rather than in allegiance to a privileged few who sit on the nation's wealth. Where leaders have been elected, they are often more respected and they represent the interests of the whole country in a way that an hereditary monarch cannot. In this modern age, you would like to see a President who has been appointed because they are the best person to represent the nation's interests (rather than because they happen to be the first son in line).

Character Profile 5: Taxpayer on a low income

As a low-paid worker, you barely earn enough to make ends meet at the end of each month, so the money you pay in tax is very precious to you, and how it is spent is of great importance. Though the royal family may pay taxes themselves too, when there is a royal occasion – perhaps a wedding or a royal visit – the nation foots some of the bill for the events and this seems unfair. You have not been able to afford a holiday in years, yet the monarch is about to leave for a royal tour of Africa (and who will be paying?).

Character Profile 6: Tourist officer

The single biggest factor that draws in foreign tourists each year is the royal family – fact. Whether it is to visit their residencies (old and new), read their history, or attend royal events, the monarchy remains a great pull for visitors and this can only be good news for the country's tourist industry. To lose the royal family at the helm may be more democratic, more just, but thousands of people's livelihoods depend on visitors flocking to see one of the oldest and most famous family dynasties in the world.

Character Profile 7: Retired army major

When you fought in wars you fought for 'King and country.' When you gathered for ceremonies you sang the national anthem, loud and clear. You didn't do this just for the personal family members that make up the royal line; you did it for what the monarchy stands for. Having a royal family is a sign of strength, of good governance and of continuity. Like millions of others, you are proud of how your monarch has led the country through some very difficult times, always being there to support the public. They are public servants of the highest order and they deserve our respect.

Character Profile 8: Headteacher of a comprehensive school

You are keen for your pupils to understand the role that the monarchy has played in the history of the nation. The King or Queen has always been there to show support and strength, particularly in adversity. Though the members of the family themselves are not elected, it is what they stand for that is so important to a royal nation. It is like having the best china in the cupboard, or a best suit – rarely used, but indispensable when the occasion calls. Like precious heirlooms that you may not have chosen to buy for yourself, the monarchy is a national treasure, and one that millions of visitors flock to see.

Character Profile 9: Business manager

What many people don't always realise is the extraordinary reputation the royal family has overseas. As a business manager who travels abroad many times a year through work, you are proud of the quality and strength symbolized in images of the monarchy abroad. When a member of the royal family visits a country, so many links are forged – and these always include strong business links. To lose the monarchy would mean much of the country's reputation across the world would change forever.

Character Profile 10: Journalist

As a reporter you have travelled extensively throughout the world, and everywhere you go, people have always heard of the nation's royal family. They are iconic figures – representing traditional values and upholding notions of duty, honour and responsibility. Nowhere else across the world is the royal family derided in the way that it is in its own country. You feel sure that if people could see how highly the monarchy is regarded in other countries, they would never consider wiping it away: they would cherish it.

Character Record Sheet

Name.................................

Pupil name:

Character role:

Views:

Pupil name:

Character role:

Views:

Pupil name:

Character role:

Views:

Pupil name:

Character role:

Views:

Pupil name:

Character role:

Views:

Early Start

Section 1: Lesson Plans

Lesson 1

Arrange a circle meeting for the whole class. Introduce the theme for the unit by reading out the following Context Builder 13 (enclosed at the end of this unit).

Context Builder 13	Unit 13 (Year 9)
Context	A new plan is proposed to restructure the school timetable in a large comprehensive school: it is proposed that pupils will begin at 7.30am and finish at 1.30pm. All academic lessons will be finished by 11.30am each morning, with the remaining periods reserved for break, then sports and creative subjects. Clubs and activities will be offered in the afternoons, though these will be optional.
Scenario	Starting early is good news for many pupils, staff and parents – but not everyone is overjoyed at the plan. For some, the early starts will be very inconvenient, while others have rarely been out of bed before 7.30, let alone sitting in the classroom, pen in hand. A public meeting to discuss the controversial new timetable is to be held in the school hall – everyone is invited!
Glossary	*Restructure* – organise differently *Controversial* – causing disagreement among interested parties.

Begin with a brief discussion of the timetable in your school – when it begins and when it ends. Consider when the academic lessons are situated in the day. Is this deliberate?

Consider when, for the pupils, is the most productive time of the day. Is it before lunch? Why? Elicit the pupils' own feelings about when the school day should start. Is it ideal at the moment? Could it be improved?

Return to the proposed plan to change the structure of the day at the comprehensive school in this unit. Try to identify possible reasons why people might oppose such a plan. Consider the effects of such a rescheduling on the whole school community, and not just on the pupils themselves.

Move on to considering why some people may support such a plan. Are there any statistics that prove children are more productive and attentive early in the day? Consider too the needs and working arrangements of the parents – the taxi drivers who do the ferrying. What would suit them? Would they have different views from each other? What are the factors that might affect their decision to support or oppose the changes? What other commitments might they have?

When everyone has had the chance to contribute, establish the groups for the unit. You may wish to record the names in each group for future lessons. Then read out the following Character Cards (also enclosed at the end of the unit for photocopying), and give everyone a role to play.

Character Card: For   Unit 13 (Year 9)

The following characters support the proposed changes to the timetable:

Recommended characters:

- working parent
- school secretary
- literacy coordinator
- head of art
- governor (and Managing Director of a company).

Further suggestions:

head of Mathematics

head of Science

grandparent (and former teacher)

consultant child psychologist

careers advisor.

Character Card: Against   Unit 13 (Year 9)

The following characters oppose the proposed changes to the timetable:

Recommended characters:

- school caretaker
- catering manager
- head of Sport
- working parent
- peripatetic music teacher.

Further suggestions:

Year 11 pupil

university lecturer (and parent)

road safety advisor

teaching assistant (with own family)

after-school club supervisor.

Individual Character Profiles will offer each pupil a brief summary of his or her character's viewpoint in relation to the scenario – that is, how and why they will be affected by the outcome.

There are a total of ten characters available (five recommended characters from each side), though others may be added if necessary. All pupils in each group must receive a different role – and preferably half the roles will come from Character Card: For and the other half from Character Card Against.

Explain to the pupils what is to happen next: before the next workshop (Lesson 2), the pupils must spend time developing opinions and constructing arguments in note form, on behalf of their character. Each pupil will need to come to the group prepared to argue for or against the new timetable – with good reasons to support their arguments. Speakers will do well to consider the interests of the whole school community – showing how the new day will impact on everyone (rather than just themselves).

Lesson 2

Begin with a circle meeting. Revisit the vision statement, core values and group pledges of the preliminary lessons. Reiterate the importance of abiding by the pledges when interacting within the group discussions that follow. Everyone must have a chance to speak and to listen.

The pupils reform the groups from Lesson 1. Give a copy of the Character Record Sheet to every pupil. Each group member will have a turn to share their opinions and arguments in respect of the plan to start the school day at 7.30 am. Pupils will need to listen carefully to each other, noting down the names, roles and a brief two-line summary of the views of the other members in their group. Collect in the record sheets at the end of the session – and check against the original Character Profile cards.

At the end of the session, hold a short plenary in which children are invited to report back to the whole class not on their specific views and arguments, but on the process of sharing opinions – was it helpful to find others with similar views? Was there a sense of different sides forming in the group as people discovered who shared their own views and who did not? Which was easier, expressing one's own viewpoint or listening to the views of another? Did the children find themselves paying more attention to those who shared similar views to their own?

Explain to the pupils the next step in the unit – each pupil is to prepare a letter to the headteacher of the school in question (played by the teacher) in which they state their own views on the plan to change the structure of the school day. The next workshop will be a 'focus feedback' meeting hosted by the headteacher (that is, the teacher) in which some of the letters may be read out formally, after which everyone will have the chance to speak or ask questions.

Lesson 3

The lesson begins with a short group session in which pupils who are playing the same characters across the groups get together to share ideas and thoughts, and prepare a good case. They can refer to their letters for their views if they wish. Each group of 'like-characters' will need to elect a spokesperson (some one different from the spokesperson for Unit 12). The elected speaker will address the class at the following school meeting.

Come together as a class and explain the procedure for the meeting: there will be a table at the front of the room from which the fictional headteacher (the teacher) will chair the meeting. Sitting either side of the chairperson will be the elected spokespersons (one of every recommended character from the character cards: that is, five on each side). The format for the meeting can be altered to suit timings and location, but a suggested order might be:

- Chairperson (the teacher) opens the meeting with an explanation of the plan to bring the school day forward to 7.30 am and finish earlier in the afternoon.

- Chairperson invites each of the characters to present their viewpoints, beginning with a supporter of the new timetable and then alternating between supporters and opposers.

- Chairperson invites comments from the floor – this is an opportunity for other pupils to ask questions or express their views.

- Final vote – for this you will need to distil the different ideas into a shortlist of options. These might include:

  1. Approve the new plan to change the timetable and go ahead with the new changes.

  2. Recommend alterations to the new structure – for example, starting slightly later than planned, or starting early on certain regular days only etc.

  3. Agree to wait- and carry out more research, perhaps by visiting other schools in the area that have made similar changes, to see if they were successful. Also carry out a survey of staff, pupils and parents, to identify opinions.

  4. Abandon the plan to change the timetable and keep the status quo.

The different characters may well have different views – and it was very important that these were properly heard. However, once the options are listed, pupils will need to consider the question:

If I cannot have exactly what I want, what would the next best thing be?

It may be useful here to revisit the vision and core values of the preliminary lessons, to remind the pupils of the core objectives and the need for a consensus.

Lesson 4

This shorter session comprises of a class discussion (out of role), in which all pupils may feedback to the rest of the group their thoughts on the role-play. The meeting can be an informal discussion loosely based around the themes of tolerance, empathy and cooperation, or you may wish to lead the session using the following questions as a guide:

- Were people's different views based on different personal needs and commitments or on more general educational principles?

- Which were more important, the practical implications or the educational theory behind the changes – theory or practice?

- Was it possible to keep everyone happy all of the time? If not, who gained priority? Who's views were more important?

- Could everyone empathise with each other's predicaments? Could people understand why others held different views from their own, based on their own particular circumstances?

- When devising a timetable – what should the main criteria be? What are the factors that must be taken into account?

Section 2: Follow-up Activities

Letter

The decision to bring the timetable forward has been agreed provisionally by the education committee at the school. As Head teacher, your job now is to write to parents, giving them details of the final arrangements and 'selling' the idea to them so that they will support the changes when they come into effect next year. Your letter needs to be formal yet positive, informative and persuasive.

Timetable

As the Director of Studies in your school, it is your job to devise a first draft of the new timetable, following the changes now agreed. Choose at least one year group and write their new timetable, beginning lessons at 7.30 am as agreed and finishing at lunch time, with optional sports, clubs and activities in the afternoon sessions.

Prospectus

It is a whole year now since the new changes were made to the school day and, so far, they have been a success. It is time now to redesign the school prospectus – featuring the new school timings as the main 'selling point' of the school. Your job is to write the section of the prospectus that is concerned with the timetable. You will need to write a two page spread in which you describe the school timetable, giving examples of a typical day, and explaining why it is a such a success. You may include illustrations also to help create a positive impact on readers of the prospectus.

History research

How has the traditional school day evolved over the years? When did lessons begin in Victorian times for example? Has school always lasted all day? What sort of subjects were taught years ago? Do we try to squeeze in more lessons and subjects now than we used to – or do we learn less in a typical school day? Consider how the school day has become influenced by the working culture in which we now live. Do you think school has become more or less demanding?

Essays

What might a school curriculum and timetable look like in the year 2075? Will pupils still congregate in a central place as they do now? At what times might they start and finish? What will be regarded as important knowledge to be taught? What role will home computers and communication technology have in the future?

Section 3: Curriculum Overview

Curriculum Overview	National Curriculum references
Citizenship	1g, 1h, 2a-c, 3a-c
PSHE	1b, 2c, 3a-e, 3i, 3k, 4f, 4g
History	2c-d, 3a, 5a-b, 7b, 11
English	En1: 1a-g, 2b-f, 3a-b, 4a, 8a-c, 9c, 10a, 11a En2: 1c, 2h, 3a, 4c, 5b, 5d, 9a-b; En3: 1c-d, 1e-h, 1i-k, 9b-d
NLS Text Types	persuasive texts: formal letter; school prospectus chronological report: historical essay discursive text: essay on timetables in the future.

Context Builder 13	Unit 13 (Year 9)

Context

A new plan is proposed to restructure the school timetable in a large comprehensive school: it is proposed that pupils will begin at 7.30am and finish at 1.30pm. All academic lessons will be finished by 11.30am each morning, with the remaining periods reserved for break, then sports and creative subjects. Clubs and activities will be offered in the afternoons, though these will be optional.

Scenario

Starting early is good news for many pupils, staff and parents – but not everyone is overjoyed at the plan. For some, the early starts will be very inconvenient, while others have rarely been out of bed before 7.30, let alone sitting in the classroom, pen in hand. A public meeting to discuss the controversial new timetable is to be held in the school hall – everyone is invited!

Glossary

Restructure – organise differently

Controversial – causing disagreement among interested parties.

Character Card: For   Unit 13 (Year 9)

The following characters support the proposed changes to the timetable:

Recommended characters:

- working parent
- school secretary
- literacy coordinator
- head of art
- governor (and Managing Director of a company).

Further suggestions:

head of Mathematics

head of Science

grandparent (and former teacher)

consultant child psychologist

careers advisor.

Character Card: Against   Unit 13 (Year 9)

The following characters oppose the proposed changes to the timetable:

Recommended characters:

- school caretaker
- catering manager
- head of Sport
- working parent
- peripatetic music teacher.

Further suggestions:

Year 11 pupil

university lecturer (and parent)

road safety advisor

teaching assistant (with own family)

after-school club supervisor.

Character Profile 1: Working parent

As a working parent, you would like to start the day as early as possible. There have been several occasions when you have been late for work because of the traffic on the school run. If your children started even earlier, you could miss much of the usual traffic and might even arrive early for work. You only work mornings, so collecting the children earlier in the afternoon suits you well. If the planned change improves your usually manic start to the day, it can only be good news. You feel sure that your children are at their best in the morning anyway!

Character Profile 2: School secretary

As an early riser, you usually start work well before everyone else anyway, and have often wished you could get the day going sooner and then finish earlier in the afternoon. Indeed you are not alone: you often receive phone calls from frustrated parents, wanting to drop their children off at school extra early so that they can get to work. Out of your window you often see the cars queuing up, waiting for the caretaker to open the gates and the early morning duty staff to arrive.

Character Profile 3: Literacy coordinator

Experience has taught you that your pupils are certainly at their freshest first thing in the morning. The difference in their level of concentration between 9.00am and 12.30pm is quite marked. Starting even earlier would mean you would no longer have to do battle with other subject teachers over those few precious morning slots – all academic lessons would be assigned prime teaching and learning time. You can just see those quick fire spelling tests and language starters waking up the children and getting the day underway nice and promptly!

Character Profile 4: Head of art

Freeing up more time in the afternoon for extended art projects sounds a wonderful idea – rather than having to cram in extra-curricular activities during a short lunch break before academic lessons are resumed. Though the pupils do receive one full art lesson per week in the timetable, extra time in the afternoons created by the planned timetabling change would prove very productive for you. As long as you don't have to be the one teaching at 7.30am every morning, you don't mind!

Character Profile 5: Governor (and Managing Director of a company)

Business is changing, breakfast meetings and flexi-time at work are leading to earlier starts for many. The hours in the morning are often more productive, when deals are struck and money markets are most active. If such a timetabling change at school helps to prepare young adults for the early starts that may await them in their working careers, it is good news. Being able to rise early and get stuck into work quickly will certainly bring rewards in the workplace, so best to instil a good work ethic as soon as possible.

Character Profile 6: School caretaker

Starting the day earlier has benefits for many people, not least the parents who work early – you can see that from the number of parents who queue up outside the gates every morning, waiting for you to let them in; but who is the one who has to run around the school campus unlocking everywhere at the crack of dawn? It is already very difficult trying to get round the buildings in time for the early teachers, but bringing the whole timetable forward is going to mean you are getting up before you even go to bed! Perhaps they would prefer it if you slept in a sleeping bag next to the gates, or stayed on duty all night in a sentry post. Where will it end?

Character Profile 7: Catering manager

You have heard rumours that such early starts for the children may well result in the school offering a breakfast service before lessons begin, to avoid them having to rush at home. If this is true, it will be the last straw for you and your team of cooks. It is hard enough trying to prepare the morning snacks and school dinners in the time available before lunch – and that is with coming in to work early as it is. You feel sure that your staff will not like having to come in even earlier, and then having to provide breakfast before they can even begin preparing the main meal of the day.

Character Profile 8: Head of Sport

Bringing the timetable forward to make the most of the productive hours before lunch may sound great for the English and Maths teachers, but who is the one who will need to keep them awake into the afternoon? The performances of your teams may well suffer if the players have been up since the crack of dawn! You cannot bring match fixtures forward anyway and will need to keep the children at school for afternoon kick-offs. The last thing you need is a goal-keeper who falls asleep.

Character Profile 9: Working parent

The proposed timetable changes may suit some parents and staff, but as someone who works nine-to-five in an office in town, you foresee real problems ahead. Your children may well have to stay in after-school club until you can collect them and this will give them such a long day, having started at the earlier time of 7.30am. Unless you can rearrange your own working hours (which is unlikely) you may have no choice but to consider moving your children to another school – just when they are settled too.

Character Profile 10: Peripatetic music teacher

Just when will the pupils' individual music lessons fit in to this new timetable? You feel frustrated that you have not yet been consulted about something that will undoubtedly impact on your own teaching hours. Will you have to arrive at school early in the morning too? This may suit some staff, but as musician who has to supplement their income from playing in concerts and shows late into the night, an early start in school is going to be difficult.

Character Record Sheet

Name.....................................

Pupil name:	
Character role:	
Views:	

Pupil name:	
Character role:	
Views:	

Pupil name:	
Character role:	
Views:	

Pupil name:	
Character role:	
Views:	

Pupil name:	
Character role:	
Views:	

Under One Roof

Section 1: Lesson Plans

Lesson 1

Arrange a circle meeting for the whole class. Introduce the theme for the unit by reading out the following Context Builder at the end of this unit, for photocopying purposes).

Context Builder 14	Unit 14 (Year 9)

Context	A major retail giant is planning to build a hypermarket on the edge of a small market town. The planning department of the local council have received a strong planning application from the retail company and the building project looks like a possibility.
Scenario	The proposed hypermarket would bring some much-needed jobs to the area and would be such a useful resource for local shoppers. However, opinion is divided over the plan and the local council have been inundated with letters from concerned parties. The hypermarket would threaten so many small businesses locally, from butchers to bakers, chemists to DIY stores, and may even turn the market place into a ghost town.
Glossary	*Hypermarket* – a very large supermarket. *Planning Application* – a request to the council for permission to build or extend a property or premises.

Begin with a brief discussion of traditional market towns, where local tradesmen sell their wares. Compare this to today's trend for large supermarkets encompassing vast product ranges, competitively priced and located in one place.

Consider reasons why people in the local community might be in favour of the plan to build the hypermarket on the outskirts of the town. Think about residents' own circumstances – their need to find parking spaces, shop quickly and with little inconvenience. Focus particularly on this notion of convenience – is it more important than customer loyalty, or local tradition? Why should customers keep buying from one source, when another more convenient and cheaper one arises?

Consider who in the local area may have objections to the planned hypermarket. Think of those whose livelihood might depend upon residents and visitors coming in to the town centre to shop, rather than travelling out of town.

When everyone has had the chance to contribute, establish the groups for the unit. You may wish to record the names in each group for future lessons. Then read out the following Character Cards (also supplied as photocopiable sheets at the end of the unit), and give everyone a role to play.

Character Card: For | Unit 14 (Year 9)

The following characters support the plan to build the hypermarket:

Recommended characters:

- local shopper (easier to shop in one hit – convenient)
- parent with young children (easier to park up and use trolleys)
- unemployed resident (needs a job)
- town centre resident
- local builder (get everything in one place).

Further suggestions:

job centre manager

local teacher

daily commuter

parking attendant

elderly shopper.

Character Card: Against | Unit 14 (Year 9)

The following characters oppose the plan to build the hypermarket:

Recommended characters:

- local butcher (out of business)
- small business advisor (lose trade locally)
- librarian (less visitors)
- local historian (change culture of town)
- local farmer and supplier.

Further suggestions:

local resident

town planner

park attendant

history teacher

community officer.

Individual Character Profiles (at the end of this unit) will offer each pupil a brief summary of his or her character's viewpoint in relation to the scenario – how and why they will be affected by the outcome.

There are a total of ten characters available (five recommended characters from each side), though others may be added if necessary. All pupils in each group must receive a different role – and preferably half the roles will come from Character Card: For and the other half from Character Card Against.

Explain to the pupils what is to happen next: before the next workshop (Lesson 2), the pupils must spend time developing opinions and constructing arguments in note form, on behalf of their character. Each pupil will need to come to the group prepared to argue for or against the plans to build the hypermarket – with good reasons to support their arguments. Speakers will do well to consider the interests of the whole community – showing how building the giant retail outlet may affect the town and its people (rather than just themselves).

Lesson 2

Begin with a circle meeting. Revisit the vision statement, core values and group pledges of the preliminary lessons. Reiterate the importance of abiding by the pledges when interacting within the group discussions that follow. Everyone must have a chance to speak and to listen.

The pupils reform the groups from Lesson 1. Give a copy of the Character Record Sheet to every pupil. Each group member will have a turn to share their opinions and arguments in respect of the planning application. Pupils will need to listen carefully to each other, noting down the names, roles and a brief two-line summary of the views of the other members in their group. Collect in the record sheets at the end of the session – and check against the original Character Profile cards.

At the end of the session, hold a short plenary in which children are invited to report back to the whole class not on their specific views and arguments, but on the process of sharing opinions – was it helpful to find others with similar views? Was there a sense of different sides forming in the group as people discovered who shared their own views and who did not? Which was easier, expressing one's own viewpoint or listening to the views of another? Did the children find themselves paying more attention to those who shared similar views to their own?

Explain to the pupils the next step in the unit – each pupil is to prepare a letter to the planning department of the local council, in which they state their own views on the application to build the hypermarket out of town. The next workshop will be a public meeting hosted by the chief planning officer (that is, the teacher) in which some of the letters may be read out formally, after which everyone will have the chance to speak or ask questions.

Lesson 3

The lesson begins with a short group session in which pupils who are playing the same characters across the groups get together to share ideas and thoughts, and prepare a good case. They can refer to their letters for their views if they wish. Each group of 'like-characters' will need to elect a spokesperson (some one different from the spokesperson for Unit 13). The elected speaker will address the class at the following focus feedback meeting.

Come together as a class and explain the procedure for the meeting: there will be a table at the front of the room from which the chief planning officer (the teacher) will chair the meeting. Sitting either side of the chairperson will be the elected spokespersons (one of every recommended character from the character cards: five on each side). The format for the meeting can be altered to suit timings and location, but a suggested order might be:

- Chairperson (the teacher) opens the meeting with an explanation of proposed plan to build the hypermarket on the outskirts of the town.

- Chairperson invites each of the characters to present their viewpoints, beginning with a supporter of the application and then alternating between supporters and opposers.

- Chairperson invites comments from the floor – this is an opportunity for other pupils to ask questions or express their views.

- Final vote – for this you will need to distil the different ideas into a shortlist of options. These might include:

  1. Approve the application and allow building to commence.

  2. Recommend that an alternative planning application be put for a smaller supermarket to be built in a location nearer to the town centre.

  3. Pursue options of building relationships between the retail company and local tradesmen, in which they may either trade in small outlets within the hypermarket, or run franchises within the town centre, entering into joint contracts with the retail giant out of town.

  4. Say no to the planning application (and other subsequent applications) for a supermarket to built in the area.

The different characters may well have different views – and it was very important that these were properly heard. However, once the options are listed, pupils will need to consider the question:

  If I cannot have exactly what I want, what would the next best thing be?

It may be useful here to revisit the vision and core values of the preliminary lessons, to remind the pupils of the core objectives and the need for a consensus.

Lesson 4

This shorter session comprises a class discussion (out of role), in which all pupils may feedback to the rest of the group their thoughts on the role-play. The meeting can be an informal discussion loosely based around the themes of tolerance, empathy and cooperation, or you may wish to lead the session using the following questions as a guide:

- Were we able to separate our individual ideals from that which is good for the town as a whole?

- Was it all ultimately about convenience? Are there more important things, like tradition, history, community?

- In real life, emotions would run high over this dilemma, because it involves so many people's livelihoods. What do you think would happen in real life?

- Which course of action would benefit the most people do you think?

- Are some people's arguments more serious than others? Does this mean some people in the community are more important than others?

- Should livelihood take precedence over convenience?

Section 2: Follow-up Activities

Radio script

As a script-writer, you have been commissioned to write a thirty-second radio advertisement for the new supermarket opening soon on the edge of the town. The advert will be played on local radio stations in the region. The advert will need to contain all the important information (opening date, services and products, hours of opening). Be persuasive and catchy, to engage listeners' interest (competitive prices, conveniently located and well set out etc.). Play out thirty seconds on your watch to identify how long the time is, and then time each draft until your script is exactly thirty seconds long.

Debate Speech

Write a debate speech proposing or opposing the following motion:

> *This House believes that large supermarket chains have single-handedly changed the face of high street shopping. They should never have been allowed to rob the small traders of their business.*

Discursive essay

As a news reporter with the local newspaper, you have been asked to write a two page feature on the controversy caused by the plans for the hypermarket. Remember to profile both sides of the story, with quotations from interested parties with conflicting views. The word limit for the piece, which may be word-processed, is 750 words. Illustrations or annotated maps and diagrams may be included.

Poems

Write two poems: one that describes the bustling market place in the centre of town before the supermarket is built; the other which depicts the same area after the large retail complex has been established out of town, leaving the market place quiet, with local businesses struggling for customers. Try to use personification, and other forms of metaphor to identify how the town's 'soul' or 'heart', which lies in the market place, is affected by the shift in business. Try to introduce contrasting tones in the two poems.

Section 3: Curriculum Overview

Curriculum Overview	National Curriculum references
Citizenship	1g, 1h, 2a-c, 3a-c
PSHE	1b, 1g, 2c, 3a-e, 3h-i, 3f-g, 4f, 4g
Geography	1a, 3a, 3c-d, 4a-b, 6gii-iv
English	En1: 1a-g, 2b-f, 3a-b, 4a-c, 6d, 8a-c, 9a-c, 10a-b, 11a-b; En2: 1c, 2h, 3a, 4c, 5d, 9a-b; En3: 1d, 1e-g, 1i-k, 9a-d
NLS Text Types	Playscripts: radio advertisement persuasive text: debate speech discursive texts: profiling local opinion poetry: descriptive, figurative verse.

Context Builder 14	Unit 14 (Year 9)

Context

A major retail giant is planning to build a hypermarket on the edge of a small market town. The planning department of the local council have received a strong planning application from the retail company and the building project looks like a possibility.

Scenario

The proposed hypermarket would bring some much-needed jobs to the area and would be such a useful resource for local shoppers. However, opinion is divided over the plan and the local council have been inundated with letters from concerned parties. The hypermarket would threaten so many small businesses locally, from butchers to bakers, chemists to DIY stores, and may even turn the market place into a ghost town.

Glossary

Hypermarket – **a very large supermarket.**

Planning Application – **a request to the council for permission to build or extend a property or premises.**

Character Card: For Unit 14 (Year 9)

The following characters support the plan to build the hypermarket:

Recommended characters:

- local shopper (easier to shop in one hit – convenient)
- parent with young children (easier to park up and use trolleys)
- unemployed resident (needs a job)
- town centre resident
- local builder (get everything in one place).

Further suggestions:

job centre manager

local teacher

daily commuter

parking attendant

elderly shopper.

Character Card: Against Unit 14 (Year 9)

The following characters oppose the plan to build the hypermarket:

Recommended characters:

- local butcher (out of business)
- small business advisor (lose trade locally)
- librarian (less visitors)
- local historian (change culture of town)
- local farmer and supplier.

Further suggestions:

local resident

town planner

park attendant

history teacher

community officer.

Character Profile 1: Local shopper

The planned hypermarket will make shopping a much more tolerable experience – and in half the time too. Being able to buy everything from groceries to nails and screws will save so much time. There will be acres of parking space too, compared to the few spaces available on the side of the road in the town centre. Though you have sympathy for the small businesses that may lose some trade, the convenience of shopping at the new place will make it just too tempting to resist.

Character Profile 2: Parent with young children

Driving round and round the crowded town centre, trying to find somewhere to park so that you, and your army of small children, can shop for groceries is a frustrating experience, to say the least. News of the large supermarket to be built on the edge of the town brings light relief. There will be plenty of larger bays, specially designed for parents with pushchairs, and there will even be a café where you can rest! The narrow pavements, the few parking spaces, and the number of steps and curbs in the town centre are not exactly welcoming for parents like yourself.

Character Profile 3: Unemployed resident

With the new hypermarket will inevitably come many new jobs, of all different kinds. You have struggled to find employment in the area for some time now and this is welcome news indeed. As soon as the advertisements appear, you will get your job application in and, with luck, will start earning money again soon.

Character Profile 4: Town centre resident

Living in the town centre has its advantages, but trying to find a parking space is definitely a challenge, with so many visitors clogging up the streets, trying to find somewhere to shop. If the hypermarket were to be built on the outskirts of the town, this would mean fewer shoppers in the town centre and fewer cars taking spaces that should be reserved for residents. You may also have the town centre shops all to yourself! Peace at last.

Character Profile 5: Local builder

You hear news that the hypermarket will have a vast DIY section, where you will be able to purchase many of the items that you use. You don't mind travelling around to specialist suppliers for certain things, but it is the common screws and nails that you always run out of! Now you can stock up during the weekly shop, and, with luck, the prices might be better too than at the little DIY store in town.

Character Profile 6: Local butcher

The butcher's shop that you run has been in your family for three generations. You enjoy an excellent reputation locally for offering fine quality fresh produce, locally supplied and competitively priced. However, you just cannot compete with giant supermarket chains who buy and sell meat on such a vast scale that their prices may well be a fraction of your own. The convenience too of being able to buy groceries in one place may also draw your customers out of town. This is the worst news your business could have received.

Character Profile 7: Small business advisor

The small businesses in the town's market place rely heavily on the good will and loyalty of local customers. Though their prices may be slightly higher, they offer excellent services and fine quality products. However, as an expert in building and maintaining small businesses, you know well that if one thing poses a serious threat to the soul trader, it is the giant force of the supermarkets. This news may well just tip some smaller businesses into the red, changing the character of the town centre for good, and putting others off the idea of setting up their own business at all.

Character Profile 8: Librarian

The little library just behind the market place has been running for nearly one hundred years. For the patrons who use it, it is a life-line and a local treasure. However, the library relies on the fact that many shoppers are already in town to shop, and they pop in to return and borrow books while they are in the area. If people choose to go elsewhere for their groceries, will they still bother to make a special trip into town to use the library? It seems unlikely.

Character Profile 9: Local historian

The town's market place has changed little in the fifty years. Many of the shops are still there, some still in the same family even. The cobbled square, on which the weekly food market still trades is becoming quite a tourist attraction. The whole area remains very much at the heart of the market town. It would be a travesty if visitors started to disappear, preferring the convenience and prices of a large, modern supermarket out of town. The thriving historic market place may soon become a shadow of its former glory – and the whole town will lose its soul. And all because beans are cheaper up the road?!

Character Profile 10: Local farmer and supplier

You have been supplying the local traders with meat and groceries for years. You have a good relationship with the shop owners and together you provide local people with first class, locally grown organic produce. You worry that not all supermarkets are so concerned about buying locally and they may well look further afield, or offer you a pittance for your own produce. Will this mean the end of an era for farmers like yourself?

Character Record Sheet

Name.....................................

Pupil name:

Character role:

Views:

Pupil name:

Character role:

Views:

Pupil name:

Character role:

Views:

Pupil name:

Character role:

Views:

Pupil name:

Character role:

Views:

Brave New World

Section 1: Lesson Plans

Lesson 1

Arrange a circle meeting for the whole class. Introduce the theme for the unit by reading out the following Context Builder 15.

Context Builder 15	Unit 15 (Year 9)
Context	People say the world is changing, and with it are attitudes to war and conflict. The need for such large armies seems to be slowly fading as relations between countries improve and pledges are made to work together for peace. Where wars do arise they are fought using technological firepower, rather than with troops on the ground alone. It is time for the country to take the next step to peace – it has pledged to reduce its armies substantially and to limit its nuclear capabilities by a significant margin.
Scenario	Many believe that the decision to reduce the country's defences is a brave and noble one, which will lead to many other nations around the world doing the same. The public money that will be saved will come in very useful too, in other areas of public spending. Yet others believe that it is a foolhardy and irresponsible course of action, leaving us vulnerable to rogue attacks from countries and leaders who may not share our vision of a peaceful, non-nuclear world.
Glossary	*Troops* – individual soldiers on the ground. *Nuclear capabilities* – a country's nuclear weapons.

Begin with a brief discussion of our armed forces: their role in today's world, both at home and around the globe.

Consider how conflicts have changed in the last few decades. Are wars fought in the same way that they were fifty years ago? Are there some similarities and some differences? Consider the many new advances in field technology – how computers and satellite systems enable hostilities to be waged from great distances. Do we actually need as many troops as we once did? Is it more about air power now? Or perhaps both?

Think about the threat posed by nuclear weapons. Does possession of nuclear capabilities act as a deterrent to others or does it make the world a more dangerous place? Is it safer to have a range of weapon systems at your disposal just in case?

Consider the moral duties of our government: firstly to spend public money in the best way possible, on things that we actually need, without investing in surpluses; secondly the responsibility our country has to show others that nuclear and chemical weapons must never be used – that the world would be a safer place without them. Consider who might propose and oppose this plan to reduce our national defences.

When everyone has had the chance to contribute, establish the groups for the unit. You may wish to record the names in each group for future lessons. Then read out the following Character Cards (also enclosed at the end of this unit and give everyone a role to play.

Character Card: For	**Unit 15 (Year 9)**

The following characters support the plan to reduce the country's defences:

Recommended characters:

- school head teacher
- hospital manager
- parent with young children
- military historian
- campaigner for environmental issues.

Further suggestions:

business consultant

former foreign diplomat

ICT expert

parent of young soldier

campaigner for world peace.

Character Card: Against	**Unit 15 (Year 9)**

The following characters oppose the plan to reduce the country's defences:

Recommended characters:

- ex-soldier
- parent with older children
- military expert
- school careers advisor
- lecturer in politics.

Further suggestions:

war veteran

retired civil servant

overseas businessman

parent of soldier

army liaison officer.

Individual Character Profiles (at the end of this unit) will offer each pupil a brief summary of his or her character's viewpoint in relation to the scenario – how and why they will be affected by the outcome.

There are a total of ten characters available (five recommended characters from each side), though others may be added if necessary. All pupils in each group must receive a different role – and preferably half the roles will come from Character Card: For and the other half from Character Card Against.

Explain to the pupils what is to happen next: before the next workshop (Lesson 2), the pupils must spend time developing opinions and constructing arguments in note form, on behalf of their character. Each pupil will need to come to the group prepared to argue for or against the programme to reduce our armed forces – with good reasons to support their arguments. Speakers will do well to consider the interests of the whole community – showing how reducing our military capabilities may affect the country as a whole (rather than just themselves).

Lesson 2

Begin with a circle meeting. Revisit the vision statement, core values and group pledges of the preliminary lessons. Reiterate the importance of abiding by the pledges when interacting within the group discussions that follow. Everyone must have a chance to speak and to listen.

The pupils reform the groups from Lesson 1. Give a copy of the Character Record Sheet to every pupil. Each group member will have a turn to share their opinions and arguments in respect of the plan to reduce our defences. Pupils will need to listen carefully to each other, noting down the names, roles and a brief two-line summary of the views of the other members in their group. Collect in the record sheets at the end of the session and check them against the original Character Profile cards.

At the end of the session, hold a short plenary in which children are invited to report back to the whole class not on their specific views and arguments, but on the process of sharing opinions – was it helpful to find others with similar views? Was there a sense of different sides forming in the group as people discovered who shared their own views and who did not? Which was easier, expressing one's own viewpoint or listening to the views of another? Did the children find themselves paying more attention to those who shared similar views to their own?

Explain to the pupils the next step in the unit – each pupil is to prepare a letter to their local MP in which they state their own views on the plan to reduce the nation's defences. The next workshop will be a 'focus feedback' meeting hosted by the local MP (that is, the teacher) in which some of the letters may be read out formally, after which everyone will have the chance to speak or ask questions.

Lesson 3

The lesson begins with a short group session in which pupils who are playing the same characters across the groups get together to share ideas and thoughts, and prepare a good case. They can refer to their letters for their views if they wish. Each group of 'like-characters' will need to elect a spokesperson (some one different from the spokesperson for Unit 14). The elected speaker will address the class at the following focus feedback meeting.

Come together as a class and explain the procedure for the meeting: there will be a table at the front of the room from which the local Member of Parliament (the teacher) will chair the meeting. Sitting either side of the chairperson will be the elected spokespersons (one of every recommended character from the character cards: i.e. five on each side). The format for the meeting can be altered to suit timings and location, but a suggested order might be:

- Chairperson (that is, the teacher) opens the meeting with an explanation of the government's proposals to make cut backs in the armed forces.

- Chairperson invites each of the characters to present their view points, beginning with a supporter of the proposals and then alternating between supporters and opposers.

- Chairperson invites comments from the floor – this is an opportunity for other pupils to ask questions or express their views.

- Final vote – for this you will need to distil the different ideas into a shortlist of options. These might include:

  1. Approve proposals and encourage the government to go ahead with their cut back plans.

  2. Recommend alterations to the plan, so that fewer cuts are made.

  3. Delay the proposals until further consultation has taken place with other nations to obtain their assurances that they will follow suit and make similar adjustments to their military capabilities.

  4. Reject the plans completely and recommend that if the government wishes to cut public spending, it looks elsewhere, outside the Ministry of Defence.

The different characters may well have different views – and it was very important that these were properly heard. However, once the options are listed, pupils will need to consider the question:

If I cannot have exactly what I want, what would the next best thing be?

It may be useful here to revisit the vision and core values of the preliminary lessons, to remind the pupils of the core objectives and the need for a consensus.

Lesson 4

This shorter session comprises of a class discussion (out of role), in which all pupils may feed back to the rest of the group their thoughts on the role-play. The meeting can be an informal discussion loosely based around the themes of tolerance, empathy and cooperation, or you may wish to lead the session using the following questions as a guide:

- Can the needs of a single country be different to the needs of the world?

- Should government's of a nation look beyond their own country's needs and circumstances?

- How do you think it is possible to achieve global consensus?

- Will there always be someone or some nation who declines to participate in global initiatives? If so, how do you get them on side?

- Can you think of other situations in life when if one person jumps others would – but no-one wants to be first?

- Just because a battalion of troops may not have seen action for some time, is that a good enough reason to disband them? How do we know they will not be needed in the future? What about tradition?

Section 2: Follow-up Activities

Journalistic Report

The decision to scale down our military might has been taken and soon many famous battalions will begin to be disbanded. As a reporter with a national newspaper, you have been given the task of running with the news as a front page item. Decide on a suitable headline and write a report of the cuts to be made – profiling different views on the proposals and then featuring an editorial comment at the end.

Debate Speech

Write a debate speech proposing or opposing the following motion:

This House believes that our nation's defences are a burden on public money and should be scaled down.

Diary entry

As a soldier in one such battalion that has been chosen to be disbanded, you are justifiably frustrated and disappointed. Describe the first day when the news comes through about the cuts. How do you and your fellow soldiers feel about the decision?

Write down your feelings in diary form.

Letter

As a former soldier, you are strongly opposed to the proposals to make cuts at the Ministry of Defence. A national newspaper is running a feature in which readers are invited to write in with their views. You decide to write such a letter. Remember that your words may be read by a great many different people across the country. You will need to put your argument across in a clear, coherent and persuasive manner so that people will support you.

Section 3: Curriculum Overview

Curriculum Overview	National Curriculum references
Citizenship	1g, 1h-i, 2a-c, 3a-c
PSHE	1g, 2f-g, 3a-e, 3h-k, 4f, 4g
English	En1: 1a-g, 2b-f, 3a-b, 4a, 6d, 8a-c, 9c, 10a-10b, 11a; En2: 1c-d, 2h, 3a, 4c, 5c, 9a-b; En3: 1d, 1e-g, 1i-k, 9b-d
NLS Text Types	Journalistic report Formal letter Chronological recount: fictional diary Persuasive text: political debate speech.

Context Builder 15	Unit 15 (Year 9)

Context

People say the world is changing, and with it are attitudes to war and conflict. The need for such large armies seems to be slowly fading as relations between countries improve and pledges are made to work together for peace. Where wars do arise they are fought using technological firepower, rather than with troops on the ground alone. It is time for the country to take the next step to peace – it has pledged to reduce its armies substantially and to limit its nuclear capabilities by a significant margin.

Scenario

Many believe that the decision to reduce the country's defences is a brave and noble one, which will lead to many other nations around the world doing the same. The public money that will be saved will come in very useful too, in other areas of public spending. Yet others believe that it is a foolhardy and irresponsible course of action, leaving us vulnerable to rogue attacks from countries and leaders who may not share our vision of a peaceful, non-nuclear world.

Glossary

Troops – individual soldiers on the ground.

Nuclear capabilities – a country's nuclear weapons.

Character Card: For

The following characters support the plan to reduce the country's defences:

Recommended characters:

- school head teacher
- hospital manager
- parent with young children
- military historian
- campaigner for environmental issues.

Further suggestions:

business consultant

former foreign diplomat

ICT expert

parent of young soldier

campaigner for world peace.

Character Card: Against

The following characters oppose the plan to reduce the country's defences:

Recommended characters:

- ex-soldier
- parent with older children
- military expert
- school careers advisor
- lecturer in politics.

Further suggestions:

war veteran

retired civil servant

overseas businessman

parent of soldier

army liaison officer.

Character Profile 1: School head teacher

The decision to lead the way in reducing the country's nuclear arsenal and so pledging to maintain peace is a brave and noble one that sets a fine example to you students, who will, after all, be inheriting the world from previous generations. As a head teacher you would like to see the younger generation enjoy a century that is free of war and released from the threat of nuclear action that has hung over our heads for so long. If reducing our own capabilities brings others a step closer to doing the same then it is good news for generations to come.

Character Profile 2: Hospital manager

Morally, the idea of reducing our defences is a brave one. What it will mean practically is more public money becoming available and this is good news for the health service. Rather than building stocks of nuclear weapons, we should be building stocks of medical equipment and addressing the very real needs that exist in so many under-funded hospitals. This plan is a good one for many different ethical, moral and practical reasons. Let's hope the government see it through.

Character Profile 3: Parent with young children

As a parent with young children, you would like to believe that the government is acting in a responsible way when it comes to shaping the world your children will inherit. This plan is a step in the right direction and will hopefully lead to other nations following suit. You will be proud to say to your children when they are older that it was this country that led the way to a nuclear-free world where wars were a thing of the past.

Character Profile 4: Military historian

As an expert in the field of military conflict and power, you know well that wars are no longer fought in the way they once were. It does seem needless to you for the country to be paying for so many troops to be trained each year, many of whom will, with luck, never see frontline action. It is a brave step to reduce the country's defences in this way but it is exactly what is needed – on moral grounds but also in economic terms. It just is not cost effective to recruit and retain troops in the way we used to.

Character Profile 5: Campaigner for world peace

The plan to reduce the country's nuclear capabilities in this way is the sort of news you have been awaiting for so long. It takes a brave nation to make the commitment to reduce its own arsenals for others to follow suit. It seems hypocritical for us to dictate that certain other countries must not be allowed to build up stocks of nuclear and chemical weapons when we ourselves are doing the same. This is a brave step on the road to peace. Let's hope the government see it through.

Character Profile 6: Ex-soldier

As former soldier you are proud of the country's long tradition of military might. It is precisely because we have such fine armed forces with the most advanced weapon systems that we are safe and secure from invasion. Our defences are the greatest deterrent to potential foe. You worry that reducing them in this way, though it may be a noble gesture and a brave step, leaves us open to attack in a way that we never were before. In today's volatile world we should be maintaining the best possible defences rather than reducing them.

Character Profile 7: Parent with older children

Your own father and brother were both in the forces and you regard life in the army as a potentially fine career, with many opportunities to travel and see the world. If either of your older children expressed a wish to join up you would be nervous but would agree to it. However, if the government goes ahead with its plan to reduce the number of troops by such a margin, one wonders if there will be any job opportunities left in the military.

Character Profile 8: Military expert

As an expert in weapon systems and troop deployment, you have studied carefully the way in which wars have been fought over the last few decades. Though it is true that fewer actual troops are needed on the ground, soldiers and armoured vehicles are still a crucial part of any battle plan and you worry that the government may have got their calculations wrong. It will only take two small conflicts in different countries to kick off at the same time and our troops will be over-stretched. Plus, you worry that the idea of reducing our nuclear capabilities at a time when the world is anything but stable is more foolhardy than brave.

Character Profile 9: School careers advisor

You have seen a number of teenagers enter the armed forces over the last few years and they have thrived. The disciplined routine, combined with the camaraderie and opportunities to travel extensively have kept young adults on a straight course, when perhaps some of them may have got themselves into trouble. With the major cuts planned, such career opportunities will inevitably be reduced and this is a pity. You can see several pupils at present who might benefit from a spell in the army, but there may not be jobs for them when they leave school next year.

Character Profile 10: Lecturer in politics

You celebrate the government's wish to lead the world in nuclear disarmament, yet as an expert in politics of the world, you feel sure that relations between countries simply don't work like that. If a country wants to reduce its defences it will do. If it does not, it won't, regardless of what another country across the globe decides to do. To achieve global consensus it is safer to enter into talks first, and then see if other countries will come on board, before we stick our necks out and expect others to follow our example. Why should they after all?

Character Record Sheet

Name.....................................

Pupil name:	
Character role:	
Views:	

Pupil name:	
Character role:	
Views:	

Pupil name:	
Character role:	
Views:	

Pupil name:	
Character role:	
Views:	

Pupil name:	
Character role:	
Views:	

Bibliography

Barnes (1992) 'The Role of Talk in Learning' Norman (ed) (1992) *Thinking Voices,* London: Hodder & Stoughton

Bruner, J.S. (1990) *Acts of Meaning,* Harvard University Press

Corson, D. (1988) *Oral Language Across the Curriculum,* Clevedon: Multilingual Matters Ltd.

DfEE (1998) The National Literacy Strategy – Framework for Teaching London: DfEE Publications.

DfEE (1999) The National Curriculum Key Stages 1 and 2 London: DfEE Publications.

DfEE (1999) The National Curriculum Key Stages 3 and 4 London: DfEE Publications.

Docking, J. (1996) *Managing Behaviour in the Primary School,* London: David Fulton Publishers Ltd.

Dornyei, Z. & Murphey, T. (2003) *Group Dynamics in the Language Classroom,* Cambridge: Cambridge University Press.

Furlong, A. (1993) *Schooling for Jobs: Changes in the Career Preparation of British School Children,* Avebury: Aldershot.

Howe, (1993) Home experience and the classroom discipline problems that can arise when needed skills are lacking in Varma, V. P. (ed) (1993) *Management of Behaviour in Schools,* London: Longman Group UK Limited.

Huddleston, T. & Rowe, D. (2003) Citizenship and the Role of Language in Gearon, L. (ed) (2003) *Learning to Teach Citizenship in the Secondary School,* London: RoutledgeFalmer

Jackson, P. (1994) Life in Classrooms in Pollard, A & Bourne, J (ed) (1994) *Teaching and Learning in the Primary School,* London: Routledge

Jerome, Hayward and Young (2003) Professional Development in Citizenship Education in Gearon, L. (ed) (2003) *Learning to Teach Citizenship in the Secondary School,* London: RoutledgeFalmer

Labov, W. (1969) The logic of nonstandard English cited in Wood, D. (1988) *How Children Think and Learn,* Oxford: Blackwell Publishers Ltd.

Vygotsky, L.S. (1978) Mind in Society: The Development of Higher Psychological Processes, Cambridge, MA, Harvard University Press, cited in Mercer, N. (2000) *Words & Minds.* London: Routledge

Wales, J. & Clarke, P. (2005) *Learning Citizenship: Practical teaching strategies for secondary schools,* London: RoutledgeFalmer